W9-CHL-485

THE COLLEGE TUITION SPIRAL

An Examination of Why Charges Are Increasing

Arthur M. Hauptman
with
Jamie P. Merisotis

a report to

The College Board
and the
American Council on Education

Copyright © 1990 The American Council on Education and
The College Board.

All rights reserved. No part of this book may be reproduced or transmitted in
any form or by any means, electronic or mechanical, including photocopying,
recording, or by any information storage and retrieval system, without
permission in writing from the Publisher.

American Council on Education   The College Board
One Dupont Circle   45 Columbus Avenue
Washington, D.C. 20036   New York, NY 10023

This publication was prepared on an Apple Macintosh using Microsoft Word
and Aldus Pagemaker software.

Copies of this book are available from Macmillan Publishing Company.
866 Third Avenue, New York, NY 10022.

The College Board and the acorn logo are registered trademarks of the
College Entrance Examination Board.

Library of Congress Catalog Card Number: L.C. 90-60987

Printed in the United States of America

printing number
1 2 3 4 5 6 7 8 9 10

TABLE OF CONTENTS

LIST OF TABLES

LIST OF CHARTS

FOREWORD

In the 1980s, the price of a college education became a sensitive issue for educators and policy makers as well as students and parents. Debate on why college tuitions are increasing and what can and should be done about it will continue in the 1990s.

In response to the many questions we encounter on the subject, we decided more than a year ago that it was important for this issue to be investigated in depth, and we both asked Art Hauptman, an expert on financing higher education, to undertake such a study as a joint endeavor of the College Board and the American Council on Education (ACE).

We believe the resulting report is the most comprehensive and penetrating analysis of the college cost dilemma to date. The study does not represent an official position of either the College Board or ACE. Instead, it is a report to our two organizations sponsored with the hope that an independent analysis would yield useful insights into a very complex public policy issue.

For the public and the media, the question is likely to be: What is the bottom-line reason for the college price spiral? The report identifies a number of hypotheses, each of which is found by the subsequent analysis to have something to contribute to the argument. But the bottom-line is that there is *no* overarching explanation. As the report notes, American colleges and universities are extremely diverse in size, location, physical plant, governance, personnel and financial practices, commitment to research, and student aid policies. These and other variables influence the amount charged by any particular institution in a given year and the rate of increase in that institution's charges over time. Relying necessarily on aggregate national data, the report suggests broad trends but does not purport to apply equally to all institutions.

Distinctly different reasons and patterns do emerge for the different sectors of higher education. The report suggests that the most important influence on tuition growth in the public sector is the fluctuating revenue outlook in each state; the more strapped the state is for revenues, the more likely tuition is to go up in public institutions. In private colleges and universities, by contrast, the report contends "that many institutions in the 1980s began increasing their tuitions to pay for improved facilities and services, higher faculty salaries, and more student aid, rather than competing for students by lowering prices and offering fewer services of diminished quality."

The report also speculates that a major factor behind the price spiral in both the public and private sectors may have been the decline in the traditional college-age group in the 1980s and the effect this demographic trend has had on enrollment trends, the costs of recruiting and retention, and the supply and demand for college graduates. This and many of the other interesting findings in the report, however, must remain speculations pending further research to determine their validity. In that sense, this report is best viewed as a starting point for addressing the issue of why college charges and expenditures are increasing, and what can and should be done about it.

Many people contributed to this effort. Art Hauptman wrote the report. Jamie Merisotis researched and prepared all of the tables and charts and also wrote the bibliography that appears as Appendix B. Larry Gladieux, executive director of the Washington office of the College Board, convened a panel of higher education experts to advise on the development of the report. The review panel included David Breneman, Carol Frances, Lucie Lapovsky, Michael O'Keefe, James Scannell, and Julianne Thrift. Each offered very helpful suggestions on the organization and the content of the report. A number of other college officials and higher education analysts saw early drafts of the manuscript, or portions of it, and also made useful suggestions and comments. We thank all those who so contributed. None of the reviewers, however, bears responsibility for any error of fact or interpretation.

College Board and ACE staff members who advised and assisted in the project include Charles Andersen, Elaine El-Khawas, Janet Hansen, Hal Higginbotham, Gwen Lewis, Haskell Rhett, and Pat Smith. Paul Wolman and Wendy Bresler edited the manuscript. Frank Klassen shepherded it through the process of desktop publishing.

DONALD M. STEWART   ROBERT H. ATWELL
President   *President*
The College Board   *American Council on Education*

Chapter 1

OVERVIEW OF TRENDS AND SUMMARY OF CONCLUSIONS

Rapid increases in college charges for tuitions, fees, and other costs of attendance have become an issue of great concern to students, parents, and policymakers. A large and growing proportion of students and their parents now worry that a college education will be out of their financial reach. Government and institutional policymakers, faced with the task of ensuring affordability, have intensified their search for ways to keep price increases down and to help families pay for college.

Representatives of higher education, government officials, and others have offered various explanations for why college charges increased at twice the rate of inflation in the 1980s, a trend in sharp contrast to the latter part of the 1970s, when tuitions and other charges grew more slowly than inflation. The pattern of tuition charges in both the 1970s and the 1980s also departs from the trend over the past half-century, during which college charges have tended to rise slightly faster--a percentage point or two per year--than the general rate of inflation.

BASIC HYPOTHESES ON THE RISE IN COLLEGE COSTS

A review of articles and statements on this issue reveals at least five categories of explanations for the rapid increase in the 1980s of tuitions and other costs of college attendance:

1. **"Colleges face increasing prices for what they purchase."** Higher tuitions and other charges reflect the increased prices that colleges are paying for the various goods and services they purchase.

2. **"Colleges are using tuition increases to finance expanded or improved services."** Colleges are purchasing more of a wide variety of services and capital needs that they are paying for at least in part through higher student charges.

3. **"The share of revenue from sources other than tuition is contracting."** College charges have increased because the share of costs covered by other nontuition revenue sources has decreased or remained stable.

4. **"Increased availability of student aid has led colleges to raise their student charges."** Expansion in federal, state, and institutional student aid makes it easier for colleges to raise their tuition charges and other costs of attendance.

5. **"Competitive pressures have convinced many colleges to increase tuitions."** Intensified competition for students and faculty has forced many institutions to increase their tuitions and other charges.

In addition to the five hypotheses listed above, this study explores another, less discussed reason why college charges have grown so fast in the 1980s: the decline in the size of the traditional college age group of 18- to 24-year-olds and the financial pressures that this demographic trend may have placed on many colleges and universities. This decline touches on many if not all of the other explanations discussed in this study, and may represent a crosscutting reason why college charges increased so much faster than inflation in the 1980s, contrary to historical trends.

In assessing these explanations, this study examines national data sources as well as available case studies of individual institutions. Although national data sources can be helpful in identifying general trends, they cannot apply equally to all institutions. American colleges and universities vary greatly in their size and location, their commitment to research, the age of their facilities, the nature of their financial arrangements with faculty and other personnel, and their student financial aid policies. These and other factors all help to determine what an institution charges and how fast those charges will increase over time. Why charges increase at one institution or at a set of institutions may differ dramatically from the reasons for increases at another institution.

Moreover, our reliance in this study on national data sources serves as a limitation because they often do not reflect the impact of institutional diversity. A more thorough testing of many of the hypotheses presented here, therefore, would require the kinds of additional research we suggest in the last subsection of this overview.

Basic data on trends in college charges and expenditures are included as Appendix A. An annotated bibliography of recent studies, reports, and data sources concerning college costs and prices is attached as Appendix B.

HISTORICAL TRENDS IN COLLEGE CHARGES

An understanding of recent trends in college costs requires some detailing of broader historical movements in what colleges charge their students, in what colleges pay for the goods and services they purchase, and in the pattern of overall incomes. It also requires some understanding of the differences between college prices, revenues, and expenditures.

Trends in college charges, other goods and services, and incomes. The recent rapid increases in college tuitions and other costs of attendance have served as a lightning rod for criticism of the American system of higher education. They also have increased parents' concern about their ability to pay for their children's education in the future. A review of these trends shows that although there is considerable basis for concern, it may be misleading to extrapolate only from the most recent and most highly publicized events.

From 1980 to 1987, tuition and fees increased by slightly less than 10 percent per year--roughly twice the rate of inflation. All college charges, including room and board as well as tuition and fees, increased at a rate of nearly 9 percent per year. The increase in college charges in the 1980s was substantially greater than price increases for other goods and services, including medical care and the price of a new home, as shown in Table 1.

The pattern of increases in college charges in the 1980s contrasts with the pattern in the 1970s, when tuitions and other charges lagged behind inflation, especially in the latter half of the decade. In the 1970s, tuitions and other

TABLE 1

CHANGES IN TUITIONS AND ALL COLLEGE CHARGES, PRICES OF SELECTED GOODS AND SERVICES, AND INCOME MEASURES, 1970 TO 1987

ITEMS	Average Annual Change (%)		
	1970-80	1980-87	1970-87
Tuition and Fees			
Public	6.1	9.0	7.3
Private	7.6	10.0	8.6
Weighted Average	6.6	9.3	7.7
College Charges			
Public	6.3	7.9	6.9
Private	7.2	9.7	8.2
Weighted Average	6.5	8.8	7.4
Income Measures			
Median Family Income	7.9	5.6	6.9
Disposable Personal Income	9.5	6.6	8.3
Adjusted Family Income	8.4	5.8	7.3
Goods & Services			
All Goods and Services (CPI)	7.8	4.7	6.5
Food	8.0	3.9	6.3
New Cars	5.2	3.8	4.7
Medical Care	8.2	8.2	8.2
New Homes	10.7	7.0	9.2
All Services	8.3	6.5	7.6
Stocks & Bonds (Total Returns)			
Common Stocks	8.4	13.8	10.6
Long Term Corp. Bonds	4.2	15.3	8.6
Long Term Govt. Bonds	3.9	14.8	8.3
U.S. T-Bills	6.8	9.0	7.7

TABLE 1 (Continued)

CHANGES IN TUITIONS AND ALL COLLEGE CHARGES, PRICES OF SELECTED GOODS AND SERVICES, AND INCOME MEASURES, 1970 TO 1987

ITEMS	Cumulative Change (%)		
	1970-80	1980-87	1970-87
Tuition and Fees			
Public	80.3	83.3	230.5
Private	107.7	95.0	305.0
Weighted Average	90.3	86.0	254.1
College Charges			
Public	84.2	70.0	213.1
Private	99.7	91.7	282.8
Weighted Average	87.6	80.2	238.1
Income Measures			
Median Family Income	113.1	46.8	212.7
Disposable Personal Income	148.4	56.2	288.1
Adjusted Family Income	123.2	48.0	230.4
Goods & Services			
All Goods and Services (CPI)	112.2	37.9	192.7
Food	115.8	30.7	182.1
New Cars	66.6	30.2	116.9
Medical Care	120.5	74.1	283.8
New Homes	176.1	61.0	344.4
All Services	122.3	55.2	245.0
Stocks & Bonds (Total Returns)			
Common Stocks	124.6	147.6	456.2
Long Term Corp. Bonds	50.6	171.5	308.9
Long Term Govt. Bonds	46.6	163.5	286.3
U.S. T-Bills	92.5	82.8	251.9

SOURCES:

College Charges: U.S. Department of Education, *Digest of Education Statistics, 1988.*

Income Measures: U.S. Department of Commerce, Bureau of the Census, *Current Population Reports*, Series P-60 (Median Family Income); U.S. Dept of Commerce, Bureau of Economic Analysis (Disposable Personal Income); Congressional Budget Office, *Trends in Family Income: 1970 to 1986* (Adjusted Family Income).

Goods and Services: U.S. Government Printing Office, *Statistical Abstract of the United States*, 1988.

Stocks and Bonds: Ibbotson Associates, Inc., *Stocks, Bonds, Bills, and Inflation: 1989 Yearbook.*

charges grew more slowly than the the price of most other goods and services. If one looks at trends since 1970, college charges are in the middle of the pack of price increases. That is, they increased more rapidly than the price of food, new cars, and all services, but more slowly than the price of medical services and new homes.

The severity of recent increases in college charges also is apparent when they are compared with the growth in incomes, which can be used as a measure of changes in families' ability to pay for college. As Table 1 indicates, increases in tuitions and all charges from 1980 to 1987 far outpaced the growth in median family income, family income adjusted for changes in family size, and disposable personal income per capita.[1] This relatively faster growth in tuition and other charges means that families' ability to meet college costs decreased in the 1980s.

In the 1970s, in contrast, college charges grew more slowly than each measure of income shown in Table 1. When looked at since 1970, college charges increased faster than median family income and the index of adjusted family income, but slightly more slowly than disposable personal income.

Comparing increases in what it costs to send a child to college with changes in the value of stocks, bonds, and other investments is one way to examine changes in parents' ability to save for their children's educational costs. Interestingly, in the high-tuition 1980s, the pretax return on stocks and bonds increased faster than the growth in tuitions and other charges, suggesting that many parents could have kept pace with college costs if they had invested in stocks and bonds. Whereas tuitions and other college charges increased by about 80 percent between 1980 and 1987, the value of stocks and bonds more than doubled--that is, increased by more than 100 percent. In the 1970s, the return on bonds lagged behind the growth in tuitions and other charges, but stocks outperformed the increase in college charges. Once taxes are taken into account, the return on stocks and bonds is reduced, however. This tax effect helps to explain why so many parents believe that whatever savings they have will not keep pace with the increase in college costs, despite the record of the past several decades.

Much of the concern about college costs has been generated not so much by the rate of increase in tuition and other charges as by the absolute dollar amounts that are now required to pay for college. The media has fed this concern by emphasizing the tuitions, fees, and other costs of attendance at the highest-priced institutions. It is not unusual for a story on college costs to begin by stating that a four-year college education now costs in excess of $80,000, based on what the most expensive private colleges and universities charge.

Yet the media tends to understate or ignore the fact that tuitions at most colleges and universities are substantially less than what the most expensive schools charge. In 1988-89, for example, roughly 200 institutions charged $10,000 or more in tuition and fees. But these 200 colleges and universities enrolled less than 5 percent of all full-time undergraduate students. At public four-year institutions, the average annual tuition and fees were less than $1,600 in 1988-89, and at public two-year institutions these charges were less than $800. The average tuition and fees in 1988-89 were around $1,200 at all public institutions, which enroll about 80 percent of all college students and 75 percent of all full-time students. Even at four-year private colleges and universities, the average tuition and fees in 1988-89 were less than $8,000, well short of the five-digit annual tuitions regularly reported in the press.[2]

The fact that tuition and fees and other charges in the 1980s increased twice as fast as inflation also may have been overemphasized by critics who have contended that colleges are "greedily" extracting more from consumers than overall inflation rates would indicate is fair. What this criticism ignores is the changing relationship of college charges and inflation over time.

Chart 1 indicates the annual percentage change in the Consumer Price Index (CPI), and in college charges for tuition, fees, room, and board between 1970 and 1987. One aspect of Chart 1 worth noting is that increases in college charges during the 1970s tended to lag behind shifts in inflation by a year or two, whereas in the 1980s the two tended to move together. Inflation heated up in the early 1970s, and college charges began rising faster a year or two later. The same pattern was true when inflation slowed in the mid-1970s, and again when it started to climb in the late 1970s. In the 1980s, however, increases in college charges closely paralleled changes in the inflation rate, with the annual percentage change in college charges remaining consistently about twice as large as the change in inflation.

Another trend indicated in Chart 1 is that college charges appear to move within a narrower band of change than does the general rate of inflation. Note that the peak of increases in inflation in the mid-1970s was higher than the increase in college charges, that inflation increases peaked in 1980 slightly higher than the largest percentage increase in tuitions, and that inflation increases in the 1980s were substantially lower than the percentage change in college charges. In terms of variability over time, therefore, the shifts of inflation in one direction or the other have been wider than the fluctuations in college charges.

CHART 1
ANNUAL PERCENTAGE CHANGES IN COLLEGE CHARGES
AND THE CONSUMER PRICE INDEX (CPI), 1970 TO 1987

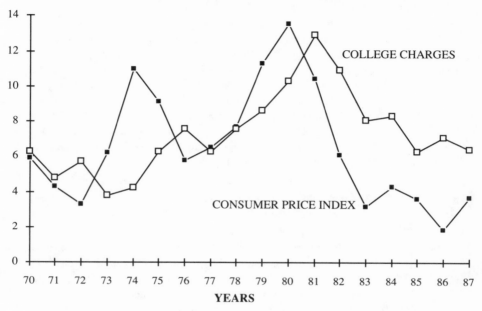

The lower volatility of tuitions and other charges relative to inflation is consistent with the fact that higher education is largely an administered price industry. A dominant characteristic of such an industry is that prices are set more by administrative fiat than by market-clearing supply and demand conditions. Other examples of administered price industries include health care, public transportation, and most heavily regulated activities. In such industries, those who set prices tend to try to smooth out variations in their underlying cost structure over time, so that extremely high inflation is not fully passed on to consumers. Similarly, large price declines for factors of production are not reflected fully in final product price cuts.

A statistical measure, the coefficient of variance, allows us to quantify the difference in the degree of variability in college charges and inflation that appears in Chart 1. This statistic divides the standard deviation of a data series by the mean of the series, thereby providing a measure of how much variation there has been around the average. Between 1970 and 1987, the coefficient of variance of the annual percentage change in college charges for public institutions was 33 percent; for private institutions, 28 percent. During that same period, the coefficient of variance for the annual change in the CPI was 49 percent. This difference in the size of the coefficient of variance confirms that inflation has been substantially more variable than the annual change in college charges, at least since 1970.

The differences between college prices, revenues, and expenditures. Any examination of college prices should include an admonition not to confuse tuitions and other charges with total institutional revenues and expenditures. Higher education is one of the few industries in our economy in which the price charged the consumer is substantially lower than the cost of producing the product, and in which the price for the product constitutes a relatively small share of total revenues. Few if any students pay the full cost of the education they receive in either the public or private sector of American higher education. For all institutions, tuition and fees represent about 20 percent of total revenues. Revenues from auxiliary enterprises, primarily room and board charges, account for slightly more than 10 percent of total revenues. Thus, all student charges combined account for about 30 percent of all institutional revenues.

These percentages differ significantly between public and private sector institutions because of the variation in their reliance on tuition and fees and state funding. In the public sector, tuition and fees from students are roughly 15 percent of total current fund revenues. For these institutions, state appropriations are a much larger source of funds than tuitions, representing 45 percent of all public sector revenues. From the perspective of tuitions as a percentage of what it costs to educate students, tuition and fee revenues are about 20 percent of education and general (E&G) expenditures at public institutions.

At private sector institutions, tuition and fees average nearly 40 percent of total current fund revenues, and are equivalent to over 50 percent of E&G expenditures. Tuitions clearly are a more important source of revenue and cover a much larger proportion of the costs of educating students at private institutions than at public ones. But other revenue sources nonetheless are still needed to pay for nearly half of the expenditures by private institutions for education and related purposes. Endowment income and private gifts represent an important source of funds for these institutions--15 percent of total revenues and 20 percent of what it costs to educate students. This income source historically has allowed private institutions with large endowments--a small percentage of all private institutions--to keep their tuitions substantially below the costs of educating students.

The fact that college tuitions do not cover educational costs fully is more than an academic statement. It affects the operations of both public and private sector institutions. In the public sector, tuitions are set as much or more by what the state provides through appropriations as by changes in costs, although cost and funding levels are clearly related. Officials at institutions with large endowments, on the other hand, can raise their prices at a different rate than the growth in their costs by adjusting expenditures from their endowments.

The difference between prices and costs also helps explain why college charges may not increase at the same rate as expenditures over time. It is perfectly plausible for college prices to increase at a different rate from expenditures because price in the form of tuition is a much smaller number than an institution's expenditure per student, or the "cost" of educating a student.

ASSESSING THE CAUSES
OF INCREASING COLLEGE CHARGES

Our review of the existing data and the literature suggests that no single explanation fully accounts for the recent growth in college tuitions. Each of the explanations discussed here has something to offer to the question of increasing college charges, depending on the focus of inquiry. Yet, as is typically the case, some hypotheses appear to be more important than others.

• The strongest factor underlying the growth of public sector tuitions, for example, seems to be the pattern of state funding. That is, when state resources are strained, public sector tuitions tend to increase more quickly than when state funds for higher education are more available.

• In the private sector, however, the preeminent cause appears to be that many institutions in the 1980s began increasing their tuitions to pay for improved facilities and services, higher faculty salaries, and more student aid rather than competing for students through lower prices and fewer services of diminished quality.

• In both sectors, the decline in the traditional college-age group in the 1980s, we believe, has been a major influence on recent tuition increases. Level enrollments have made it more difficult for institutions to spread their fixed costs over growing numbers of students, thereby contributing to pressures to raise tuitions. Increased spending for recruitment and retention of nontraditional students also has contributed to higher costs.

A summary of our main conclusions on the various hypotheses follows.

Colleges are paying more for the goods and services they purchase, including salaries and benefits for their faculty and other employees. Part of the answer to why tuitions have increased can be found in the increased prices that today's colleges and universities pay for the goods and services they purchase, as measured by changes in the Higher Education Price Index (HEPI). From 1980 to 1987, the HEPI grew at an annual rate of 7 percent, two percentage points faster than the general rate of inflation. This faster-than-inflation increase is attributable in large part to the increase in real levels of faculty and other employee compensation in the 1980s. Yet despite this real increase, faculty salaries have not fully recovered from their lag behind inflation throughout most of the 1970s.

Whether increases in faculty salaries and other employee compensation cause tuitions to rise or whether higher tuitions allow institutions to raise the pay of their employees is an important question, but one that has no neat answer. Some dramatic changes over the past decade in labor market conditions for faculty, especially in the sciences and engineering, certainly have generated additional pressure for higher salaries and other improvements in working conditions. Yet the growth in tuition revenues in the 1980s no doubt permitted institutions to improve their employee compensation more than if those additional revenues had not been available, including for faculty and other employees for whom the labor market did not materially improve in the 1980s.

The impact of higher faculty salaries on college expenditures and charges would have been even larger, however, in the absence of the trend in recent decades toward greater use of part-time faculty, especially at community colleges, which has helped to limit the increase in instructional costs. In the 1990s, some further moderation in the growth of instructional costs could occur as the large numbers of faculty hired in the 1950s and 1960s begin to retire and are replaced by younger professors commanding lower salaries.

These downward pressures on instructional costs will likely be more than offset, however, by upward pressures on salaries caused by changing labor market conditions in a number of fields. Increases in undergraduate enrollments projected to begin in the late 1990s will be accompanied by a fairly steady increase in faculty retirements and projected continued declines in the number of new PhDs. In addition, the legislatively scheduled end of mandatory retirement policies for faculty slated for the mid-1990s will moderate to some degree the rate of faculty retirements, thereby postponing the cost-reducing effect of replacing older faculty members with younger ones. Institutions will be forced to be creative in dealing with these pressures, and now may be an opportune time for them to review their tenure, contract, and recruitment policies.

The growth in instructional costs over time might have been moderated further if a wider range of colleges and universities had sought instructional productivity gains more extensively in their academic programs. For example, many research universities could have placed greater emphasis on teaching relative to the research activities of faculty, in contrast to the apparent trend toward reduced teaching loads and a heightened focus on research. Greater teaching productivity also might have been achieved through the enhanced use of new technologies. Although some institutions have been aggressive in adapting new technologies to the classroom, most have not. Many apparently are persuaded that the financial and pedagogical costs of introducing new technologies into their academic programs exceed the benefits.

Another obvious form of productivity enhancement, of course, would be to increase class sizes, although this has the substantial drawback of potentially reducing the quality of education received. The available statistics indicate, however, that overall student/faculty ratios have declined over the past decade, suggesting that most institutions in the 1980s did not seek cost efficiencies through larger class sizes.

Spending per student has increased in real terms. Current funds expenditures by colleges and universities increased 8 percent per year in the first half of the 1980s. This suggests that maintaining and improving quality through increases in the amount of goods and services purchased led to a growth in expenditures roughly one percentage point per year faster than what institutions paid for those goods and services, as measured by the 7 percent annual growth in HEPI during that time. Others have argued that the real increase in college spending was 3 percent per year in the early 1980s, by comparing the 8 percent annual growth in expenditures to the 5 percent growth in the Consumer Price Index during that time. We believe that the HEPI is the more appropriate index for measuring real changes in institutional expenditures -- that was why it was created -- and that the CPI is the better measure for gauging families' changing ability to pay for college.

Relatively level enrollments in higher education over the past decade also may have contributed to the recent rapid increase in expenditures per student. College enrollments have increased on average about 1 percent per year since the mid-1970s, in sharp contrast to the more rapid growth of the 1960s and early 1970s. For some colleges and universities, the lack of growth was the intentional result of stable-enrollment policies. For other institutions, where applicant to student ratios are much lower, level or declining enrollments may have been more a consequence of the decline in the traditional college-age population. For whatever reason, many institutions in recent years have been unable to spread their costs over a growing number of students.

One measure of the impact of level enrollments on costs is the fact that total and per-student expenditures increased at roughly the same rate between 1975 and 1985. In contrast, in the 1960s, when enrollments doubled and total spending more than tripled, per-student expenditures increased by less than 50 percent. If enrollments had continued to grow in the late 1970s and into the 1980s, the increase in per-student expenditures probably could have been reduced by one or two percentage points per year, at least at institutions that were not at full capacity and that could absorb additional students without needing additional facilities. If per-student spending had increased less, it is reasonable to suppose, the recent rapid growth in tuitions and other charges also might have slowed.

The growth of several expenditure categories merits special attention. From 1975 to 1985, the composition of spending by colleges changed very little. Instructional costs, the largest component of college expenditures in the statistics reported by the Department of Education, declined as a proportion of total spending by one to two percentage points in both the public and private sectors, whereas administrative costs increased by a similar degree. The other expenditure categories as a share of total spending remained relatively constant over the 10-year period. Although the composition of expenditures has not changed substantially since the mid-1970s, certain spending categories have increased faster than others. The fastest-growing categories have been administrative costs in both sectors, and financial aid, student services, and public service activities at private institutions.

A U.S. Department of Education report issued in 1988 suggested that bloated and overpaid bureaucracies were responsible for the rapid growth in administrative costs. But the report failed to determine how much of the growth in administrative costs might be attributed to greater student demand for services, such as career counseling and financial aid, and to greater governmental demands in affirmative action, hazardous waste disposal, and many other regulatory and reporting requirements, as opposed to unnecessary staff enlargements and excessive salary increases.

It appears that the rising costs of conducting campus-based research also may have spurred tuition increases. Even though federal support for sponsored research in the 1980s grew in real terms, the costs of doing research in the form of equipment, facilities, and salaries appear to have increased even faster, meaning in effect that institutions "lose" money with each additional federal research grant they receive. To the extent that other institutional funds are used to make up for this shortfall in federal dollars, tuitions may be "paying" for federal research. Although undergraduate tuitions have paid for graduate student fellowships for many years, tuitions now also may be supporting research operations to a greater extent than before.

The possible effects of research on tuitions are not confined to research universities alone. Faculty on most campuses have pressed for more research time funded through internal sources, and a wide range of institutions are facing pressures from accrediting bodies and others to increase their internal funding for research, especially in the professional fields of business, law, and engineering. Moreover, to the extent that research universities are frequently "price leaders" in the higher education industry, higher research costs also could be contributing to tuitions increases at nonresearch institutions.

Growing capitalization costs in the form of more computers and equipment and the construction and renovation of academic, recreational, and other facilities also may be contributing to the rise in tuitions. But the Department of Education's spending statistics are for current funds expenditures only, and therefore they do not reflect changes over time in capital investment, except in the reporting of interest expenses on debt used to finance these expenditures. If capital costs were included in the department's figures, the percentage growth in expenditures by colleges might appear larger.

State funding patterns have influenced the rate of increase in public sector tuitions. For public sector institutions in most states, changes in the availability of state resources appear to be a major reason for the pattern of tuition increases over time. The largest increases in public sector tuition and fees occurred in the early 1980s, when the annual percentage increase in tuition and fees grew at double-digit rates, much faster than inflation. During this time, the ability of states to fund public colleges and universities was constrained by the impact of the severe economic recession on state revenues, which, in turn, limited the growth in state funding for higher education. In the mid-1980s, as the economy improved, funding for higher education in most states increased in real terms, and public tuition increases have moderated.

The experience of the 1980s appears to confirm the traditional inverse relationship between economic conditions and public sector tuition increases: When the economy is in a downturn, the growth in state resources is constrained, and this in turn places greater pressure on officials to increase tuitions faster to make up for the difference between institutional budgets and the level of state funding. Conversely, when the economy improves, more state funds become available, and tuitions tend to increase less.

A principal reason for the inverse relationship between economic health and public sector tuition increases is the fact that tuitions tend to act as a buffer at the end of the budget process, making up the difference between what an institution receives from the state and its budgeted level of expenditures. It is also worth noting, with respect to the responsibility for rising tuitions, that the officials of many public colleges and universities do not set tuitions at their own institutions; that task is performed either by central governing boards or by the state legislature itself.

General economic conditions are not the only factor which affects a state's financial condition and therefore its public sector tuition levels. A state's ability to fund higher education may be constrained, for example, by increased competition between higher education and other state priorities brought about by changing federal priorities or initiatives (such as California's Proposition 13) that lead to more state responsibility for functions previously performed at the local level. If less state funding is available for higher education, tuitions may have to be increased to make up the difference between what the state provides and institutions' budgetary needs. More recently, revenue misestimates in a number of states, particularly in the Northeast, have created pressures in subsequent years to restrict funding for state activities including higher education. It is also the case that all states do not participate fully in the economic recovery. For those states with problem economies, the consequent restriction in state revenue growth forces their public sector tuitions to increase more rapidly than in most other states.

Public institutional officials also can affect revenue streams by how they set charges other than in-state tuitions. These other charges include mandatory fees, room and board charges, and tuition charges to out-of-state students. It does appear that in many states in which tuitions are set by the legislature, institution-controlled mandatory fees have increased more than tuitions. In many states, room and board charges also have increased faster than tuitions, thereby resulting in increases in total charges that exceed the growth in tuitions alone. Yet although anecdotal evidence from individual states and institutions suggests that tuitions for students from outside the state have increased faster than those for their in-state peers, available data indicates this has not been so.

At least a dozen states now have moved to a system in which their public sector tuitions are tied to a formula based on spending at public institutions or on state funding levels. In these states, public sector tuition increases tend to vary directly with changes in the economy and in state funding, rather than to follow the more traditional inverse relationship. If additional states adopt formula-based approaches to tuition setting, we should see a more direct relationship in national trends between state funding of higher education and public sector tuition increases. That is, when the states contribute more to public institutions, tuitions, by formula, will tend to rise faster than when the states' funding is more constrained.

Such a change could be beneficial in that students attending public institutions no longer would face the largest tuition increases during the leanest economic times. On the other hand, tuition/funding formulas can strain institutional budgets during times of economic recession, as revenues are reduced both because of lesser availability of state funds and lower tuition revenues. A preferable alternative would be for states and public institutions to smooth out these cyclical effects by setting up reserve funds when state funds are more plentiful to supplement the funding that is available during economic hard times. This kind of "rainy day" budgeting approach would help to protect students enrolled in public sector institutions against large-scale tuition increases such as those that occurred during the recession of the early 1980s.

Reduced income from endowments and private gifts has not been a major factor in the rapid growth of tuitions in the 1980s. The share of revenues from endowment income and private gifts, a major source of nontuition revenues for private colleges and universities, did not change appreciably between 1975 and 1985. Endowment income grew slightly as a share of all revenues, but this growth was offset by a similar reduction in the share coming from private gifts. In the public sector, there has been a rapid increase in endowments and gifts, causing concerns among private sector officials that public sector fund-raising eventually could lead to reduced endowments and gift-giving for private institutions. But endowment income and private gifts still account for a small share of the revenues of public institutions and do not appear to have much impact on their tuitions.

In discussing the role of endowments and private gifts in college financing, it is important to be aware of the great variation among institutions. The 100 colleges and universities with the largest endowments account for more than two-thirds of all institutional endowment holdings. At these institutions, fluctuations in the level of endowments and incomes often play a critical role in the setting of tuitions. But at nine out of ten institutions, annual endowment income is a small percentage of the total budget, and endowments and gifts are not significant factors in price-setting decisions.

Increased availability of federal student aid has little to do with the increase in tuitions and other charges. William Bennett, when he was secretary of the Department of Education, and other Reagan administration officials argued that the availability of federal student aid was responsible in great measure for the rapid increases in college charges in the 1980s. The premise of their argument was that many if not most colleges raise their prices because they know that federal student aid will be available to pay for these increases.

This hypothesis is flawed in at least three ways, however. First, only half of all students receive any form of federal student aid, and many receive only modest amounts. Most students, therefore, pay for tuitions themselves, and institutions cannot simply depend on federal aid to soften the blow of price increases.

Second, federal student aid increased much more rapidly in real terms in the 1970s than it did in the 1980s, whereas the growth of tuitions and other college charges was much faster in real terms in the 1980s than in the 1970s. If federal student aid were fueling tuition growth, one would expect to see a direct relation between increases in tuitions and other charges and increases in federal aid. This has not been the case. Instead, funding growth slowed noticeably in the 1980s, and the maximum grant and loan limits in federal student aid programs declined in real terms.

Third, an examination of the structure of federal student aid indicates that for the most part it does not feed tuition escalation. Grant and loan limits, as well as the mechanics of the program award formulas, prevent aid from increasing dollar for dollar with each increase in tuition and other charges. Estimates provided by the Department of Education indicate that for every dollar increase in college charges, federal student aid might increase by 20 to 30 cents for those students eligible to receive aid. When nonaided recipients are factored into the equation, a dollar increase in college charges results in perhaps 10 to 20 cents of additional aid. This represents a very weak form of indexation. It certainly does not support the theory of a strong linkage between aid and costs.

In two instances, however, the availability of federal student aid can be linked to tuition increases. At institutions that charge little or no tuition, an increase in tuition generally will be matched by a similar increase in the federal aid provided to needy recipients. The City University of New York in the mid-1970s is a case in point. The availability of federal aid also appears to influence tuition-setting in the proprietary sector. Here, the limited data that are available suggest that tuitions and other costs of attendance have moved in tandem with changes in the Pell Grant maximum award and federal student loan limits, at least at some proprietary schools.

The rapid growth of internally funded student aid has contributed to tuition increases, especially at private sector institutions. If anything, it appears that real decreases in federal student aid lead to higher prices, as many institutions have provided more aid out of their own funds in the 1980s to compensate for the slowdown in the growth of federal aid. This factor has been especially pronounced at private institutions. To the extent that this aid is paid for by increases in tuitions rather than by depletion of endowments, it adds to the "sticker price" faced by all students and their families.

Our analysis of available data indicates that the growth over time in internally funded student aid at private colleges and universities may have added from less than one to as much as two percentage points to their annual tuition increases. Although tuitions thus could have been lower if this aid had not been increased, this reduction in the sticker price would have been accomplished at the risk of less diverse student bodies and diminished access to higher education for needy students.

Many institutions, especially in the private sector, have chosen to compete not through lower prices but through expanded and improved facilities and services. In discussing the relationship between college expenditures and tuitions, it is worthwhile to distinguish between what institutions must spend and what they choose to spend. Every college and university has a basic level of expenditures it must make to keep its doors open: utilities bills must be met so that the lights stay on; faculty and other personnel must be paid sufficiently to keep them working at prescribed levels; interest on debt must be paid; creditors must be satisfied; and so on. Although revenue sources other than tuition can be used to meet these expenses, institutions must charge a certain level of tuition, as well, to meet these basic costs.

Above this minimum "base level" tuition, institutions may choose to increase their charges to pay for a variety of important projects, such as restoring the real level of faculty salaries, building new facilities or renovating old ones, providing additional financial aid to students, and enhancing student support services. The extent to which tuitions are increased determines in large measure where on the list of institutional priorities the line is drawn. The higher the tuition increase, the more items on its priority list an institution can achieve.

In the 1980s, competitive pressures in the tuition-setting process, particularly at private institutions, apparently contributed to the rapid increases in tuition and other charges. This statement seems odd since, in most industries, increased competition for customers (in this instance, students) would lead providers of a service (colleges) to *reduce* their prices. Indeed, the need to attract students by keeping prices low probably has played an important role in restraining the growth of tuition below what it otherwise would have been.

In general, however, colleges in the 1980s tended to *increase* their prices as competition for students intensified. One reason for this is that some leading institutions in the late 1970s and early 1980s apparently concluded that they were underpriced relative to their market value, and that many students and their families could and would pay more than they were being charged. This kind of pricing strategy could be justified as long as student aid budgets also were increased, so that needy students would not be denied the opportunity to attend as a result of higher sticker prices.

A number of institutions seem to have decided that they could no longer postpone renovating or replacing their deteriorating facilities, restoring the real level of faculty salaries, or meeting the demand for more student services. Many found it necessary to pay for these improvements through higher tuitions. The rapid growth in the use of internally funded student aid represents still another manifestation of competition that leads to higher prices.

Another form of competitive pressure that may have contributed to recent tuition inflation is the tendency of some institutions to follow the lead of others. That is, once price-leading institutions decided to employ a high-tuition/high-aid strategy, others followed suit. Of course, the price-leaders for one set of institutions are not the same as those for another group of institutions. Small, regional liberal arts colleges certainly do not take their lead from Harvard. But they may be influenced by what a nationally recognized liberal arts college charges, just as that school may look to the Ivy League when it sets its tuitions. Thus, the price leadership process may be propagated throughout higher education.

The pattern of tuition increases in the 1980s suggests that price leadership of this sort did occur. Large percentage increases in tuition have not been confined to a small group of expensive institutions. Instead, the pattern of rapid increases has been widespread, as institutions have tried to keep pace with the trendsetters. In a number of instances, this kind of behavior actually may have had the effect of making tuition charges a much higher proportion of per-student spending at "follower" institutions, a pattern that has led some observers to comment that in higher education, higher prices are being confused with higher quality.

Colleges also compete by providing the broadest range of course offerings and services to their students. A long-standing tendency in American higher education is to try to be comprehensive rather than to specialize in certain fields. This tradition contributes to a higher cost structure. Thus, one way to reduce costs would be for institutions to be more receptive to the notion of specialization and comparative advantage rather than aiming to be all things to all their students.

The decrease in the traditional college-age group is a crosscutting factor that helps to explain the rapid growth of tuitions in the 1980s. A common thread appears to run through many of the explanations for increasing college charges examined in this study -- the decline in the number of students in the traditional college-age group of 18- to 24-year-olds, which peaked at the beginning of the 1980s at 30 million and has since declined. There are several reasons we believe it is more than a mere coincidence that college charges began to increase so rapidly when the traditional college-age group began to decline.

At first glance, it seems the opposite effect should apply. Fewer 18- to 24-year-olds should result in fewer students going to college, and hence, as in many industries, greater pressure among competing providers to *decrease* prices for consumers. But at least three factors help to explain why the decline in the size of the traditional college age group may have resulted in pressures to *increase* prices, more than offsetting the tuition-depressing effects of the growing competition for students: (1) the higher expenditures per student that result from the inability of institutions to spread their costs over larger numbers of students; (2) increased costs for recruitment and retention; and (3) the increase in the relative economic value of a college education and its impact on demand.

The decline in the size of the traditional college age group has led to a leveling in college enrollments since the mid-1970s, after several decades of rapid increase. (Enrollments would have fallen in the 1980s except for a small increase in the participation rates of traditional college-age students and a large influx of older, nontraditional students.) As we noted earlier, these level enrollments in turn have prevented most institutions from spreading their spending increases over a larger number of students, as they did from the late 1950s through the early 1970s.

Increased recruitment and retention costs may be another result of the decline in the number of traditional college-age youth. To compete for the dwindling number of traditional college-age students, many institutions have devoted additional resources to recruitment, such as marketing efforts, larger admissions staffs, and more internally funded student aid--especially at private institutions-- to attract an adequate number of qualified students to their campuses. These recruitment costs are undoubtedly one component of the increased costs of administration that are being reported on so many campuses.

Heightened efforts to identify and attract larger numbers of minority and disadvantaged students have added not only to the costs of recruitment, but more importantly to the costs of retention as these students typically require more support services than majority students from more affluent families. The growth in the number of nontraditional and part-time students also may have resulted in increased budgetary pressures because of the additional services they require per full-time-equivalent student and the lower revenues they yield (for example, by not purchasing room and board) relative to the traditional college student. In short, college students today are a far more heterogenous group than were students of the past, and this has contributed to higher costs through the greater degree of adaptability colleges must manifest to meet these more diverse needs.

The decline in the number of traditional college-age youth probably also has contributed to the increased economic rates of return that have been reported in recent years for workers with college experience. Because a smaller number of traditional college-age students are coming out of college, employers may be competing more vigorously to hire graduates, thereby driving up the compensation these new workers receive. This heightened demand for college graduates may be one reason for the growing difference in incomes between individuals who have college training and those who do not. This renewal in the perceived relative value of a college education could well be one of the reasons for the continued high demand for a college education in the 1980s, indicated by the fact that the number of applications grew despite the decline in the college-age population. The continued growth in numbers of applicants, in turn, could be one factor that has convinced college administrators to charge higher tuitions.

College charges are likely to continue to climb faster than inflation for the foreseeable future. In the 1980s, as inflation changed, college charges moved in a similar fashion. When inflation was higher in the 1970s, however, college tuition increases did not track with inflation in a systematic way. The pattern in the 1970s suggests that if inflation increases markedly over the next several years, it probably will not be accompanied by an immediate and similar shift upward in the rate of change in college charges. Indeed, if the 1970s are a guide, a narrowing and perhaps a crossing in increased college charges and overall inflation are more likely.

To the extent that the decline in the number of traditional college-age youth played a major role in the increase in college spending and charges per student in the 1980s, as we have argued, the continued decline in this age group through the mid-1990s suggests that college charges probably will continue to outpace inflation for the foreseeable future.

Such a projection of continued rapid increases in college charges should be tempered, however, by noting that other factors could change. For example, it is difficult to imagine that consumers will be unlimited in their willingness to pay steadily rising college prices. Although demand apparently was relatively insensitive to price increases in the 1980s, basic economic theory suggests that at some point price increases at double the rate of inflation will lead to greater price sensitivity on the part of the consumer. This would be especially so if, in the future, the perceived value of a college education once again diminishes, as was the case throughout much of the 1970s.

The future course of the economy also could be an important factor in determining the pattern of tuition increases. In the public sector, an economic downturn would place greater pressure on institutions to raise their tuitions to make up for constrained growth of state funding sources, especially in the majority of states which have no direct linkage between tuition levels and institutional funding or expenditure levels. For private sector colleges and universities, an economic slowdown could threaten their high-tuition/high-aid strategy because a recession would dampen the willingness and ability of many middle- and upper-income families to pay the growing costs of attendance, thus limiting the ability of these institutions to raise their charges.

DIRECTIONS FOR ADDITIONAL RESEARCH

In preparing this report on why college charges have increased, we repeatedly encountered areas that require additional research. The areas in which more research would prove most fruitful include the following:

The rapid growth in administrative costs. Further examination of the reasons why administrative costs have increased so rapidly would be helpful. Have these costs increased simply to pay for more institutional overhead, or have they risen to meet growing student demands for more services and requirements imposed by more government regulations? Case studies could prove most useful here. Such research should take into account the enormous variation in the cost structure of different types of institutions.

The relationship of research spending and tuitions. The assertion that the additional costs of doing campus-based research have been a factor in the recent increase in undergraduate tuitions should be investigated further. It would be worthwhile to know, for example, whether institutional efforts to maintain their research structure on campus are contributing substantially to increased tuitions, or whether other nontuition revenue sources are being used to pay the increased costs of doing research. Such an analysis of cost trends might also consider whether current statistical treatment of expenditures should be modified to reflect the growing capitalization of many campuses for research and other needs.

The impact of faculty trends on instructional costs. There are many unresolved issues regarding trends in faculty compensation and utilization, and their possible impact on college expenditures and charges. For example, to what extent are changing hiring patterns affecting the cost structure of institutions? Would the introduction of new teaching technologies result in cost efficiencies, and how would it affect the quality of the education received? Will a trend toward more dependence on outcomes assessment have any substantial impact on the utilization of faculty?

The diversity in institutional circumstances. This report was limited to an examination of how *national* trends help to explain the growth in college charges. But concentrating on national data necessarily masks the different reasons why particular institutions raise their tuitions and other charges. Further research should focus on the degree to which institutional differences help to explain the pattern of tuition increases.

The composition and impact on tuitions of internally funded student aid. Relatively little data are available on the student aid that institutions provide from their own funds. The growth over time in this form of aid, whether it has been funded through higher tuitions or through the use of endowments, and what types of aid are available all remain unclear. The federal government no longer asks for this information when institutions apply for campus-based aid; this change increases the need for an alternative data source.

Additional work is needed to determine the role of internally funded student aid in recent college tuition increases.

The role of institutional pricing policies. Many questions remain about the influence of pricing policies on the rise in tuitions and other charges at both public and private institutions. Further investigation, for example, is needed of the impact on public sector tuition levels of formulas that tie tuitions to expenditure or state funding levels. Under what circumstances do these funding formulas work, and what are the limitations of such arrangements, especially when state funding is enrollment-driven as well? In addition, an analysis of the reasons for the possible divergence at public institutions in the growth of tuitions and other charges for mandatory fees and room and board would be helpful. For private colleges and universities, more work is needed to identify different pricing models that are used at the institutions. Does the type of pricing model that an institution uses have an effect on how fast its tuition increases?

The impact of enrollment trends on college charges. In this study we have speculated that the decline in the size of the traditional college-age group and the leveling in higher education enrollments have been important factors in the surge of tuitions in the 1980s. But more analysis is needed, through case studies and through more thorough examination of financial and demographic trends, to determine the extent to which this hypothesis is valid. One avenue of analysis would be to examine whether high tuition increases correlate with low enrollment growth among a cross section of institutions measured over different time intervals.

Endnotes

[1] The measure of income used makes a difference in how increases in college charges compare with changes in income over time. Median family income, for example, has grown more slowly than disposable personal income in the 1980s for a number of reasons, including the increase in two-earner families. In recognition of some of these differences, the Congressional Budget Office (CBO) in 1988 published an analysis, *Trends in Family Income, 1970-1986*, in which the median family income was converted into an index and adjusted for several factors, including principally the reduction over time in the average size of American families. Changes in the CBO index appear as the figure for adjusted family income in Table 1.

[2] Figures on tuitions and unpublished tabulations of enrollments cited here are from the College Board's "Annual Survey of Colleges" (New York: 1989).

Chapter 2

EXPLORING THE MAJOR EXPLANATIONS FOR THE RISE OF COLLEGE CHARGES

This portion of the study details our analysis of the various explanations that have been given for the rapid growth of college charges in the 1980s. We approached the analysis by pulling together five basic hypotheses on the recent behavior of college charges. We constructed these hypotheses from the comments and writings of college presidents and other administrators, as well as from the public musings of federal and state government officials, economists, and other observers. The five hypotheses are as follows:

1. **"Colleges face increasing prices for what they purchase."** Higher tuitions and other charges reflect the increased prices that colleges must pay for the goods and services they purchase, including the salaries and benefits for faculty and other employees.

2. **"Colleges are using tuition increases to finance expanded or improved services."** Colleges have increased their spending to improve the quality or increase the quantity of college and university services and capital needs, and they have paid for these expenses through higher student charges.

3. **"The proportion of revenues from nontuition sources is contracting."** College charges have increased because the share of costs covered by nontuition revenues such as state and federal funds and endowment income has decreased.

4. **"Increased availability of student aid has led colleges to raise their student charges."** The increased availability of federal and internally funded student aid has led many colleges to raise tuitions and other charges more than they otherwise would have.

5. **"Competitive pressures have convinced many colleges to increase their tuitions."** A set of competitive factors, including the need to recruit and retain good faculty and to attract and retain qualified students, has compelled many institutions to increase their tuitions and other charges to pay for enhanced facilities and services.

In addition, there is a crosscutting factor in the rapid rise in college charges in the 1980s: the decline in the size of the traditional college-age group. This demographic phenomenon, we believe, touches on many if not all of the five hypotheses discussed in this study.

While our list of hypotheses may differ from the lists offered by others, we believe that ours provides a reasonably full flavor of what is being said about the growth of college costs and can serve as a good starting point for discussion. The list also could be arranged in a different order. For example, revenue shortfalls could be discussed before addressing expenditure growth. There is no right order for discussing these issues. What we have done here is to discuss expenditure issues, then revenues, then the question of whether student aid contributes to tuition growth, and finally the role of the tuition-setting process -- where expenditure, revenue, and student aid decisions all come together.

Our assessments of the validity of these explanations are based principally on national trends, supplemented by reference to case studies of institutional finance. Thus, we have not collected new data, and we have not conducted extensive new statistical analysis of existing data. Nor have we attempted to draw distinctions among subcategories of institutions along the lines of Carnegie classification, geographical location, religious affiliation, or other characteristics.

Because of these limitations, the reader should not assume that the reasons that may apply for higher education as a whole, or for broad categories of institutions, must hold for a particular college or university. There is so much institutional variation in American higher education that probably no study-- much less a limited one such as this--could make such universally applicable claims. Instead, we have attempted to use available data to outline what appears to be happening nationwide in the setting of tuitions and other charges. Institutional administrators and others may wish to use these generalizations as benchmarks in assessing what has happened at their own institutions. Throughout this analysis, we also suggest a number of avenues for further research that may help provide a fuller understanding of a number of the issues that we raise but cannot resolve here.

"COLLEGES FACE INCREASING PRICES"

Many college and university officials have responded to concerns about recent tuition increases by citing the expenses of running an institution--the prices they pay for faculty and other personnel, equipment, construction, maintenance, utilities, and so on. The prices of these goods and services, officials say, are increasing, and these cost increases are being passed on to student consumers in the form of higher charges. This suggests simple cost-push economics. Do the facts bear out this theory?

Comparing the HEPI and the CPI. The Higher Education Price Index (HEPI) was developed by researcher Kent Halstead in the 1970s as a government statistic to measure changes over time in the price of the goods and services that colleges and universities purchase.[1] The HEPI generally receives good grades as an indicator of trends in the cost structure that colleges face in buying what they need to operate.

But the HEPI has its drawbacks and detractors as well. A principal concern has been the inclusion of salaries and benefits for faculty and other employees as the major element of the index. Because employee compensation, in effect, is internally decided by an institution, it is reasonable to argue that it should not be included in an index intended to measure externally generated price pressures. This is a legitimate concern, yet an index of higher education costs that did not include employee compensation would be embarrassingly incomplete, because it would ignore most of the underlying cost structure. It also can be argued that although compensation levels are decided by the institution, many external factors--particularly what other institutions are paying--help to determine what faculty and other employees receive for their services.

Although the HEPI is not perfect, it does reasonably measure the changes over time in what colleges and universities pay for what they purchase, and a look at the HEPI in a historical context is merited. Between 1980 and 1987, the HEPI grew by 58 percent, which translates into an average annual change of 6.8 percent, as shown in Table 2. Among the components of the HEPI, the fastest-growing in the 1980s has been fringe benefits, which more than doubled between 1980 and 1987. Several of the HEPI components increased by 50 to 60 percent between 1980 and 1987 -- roughly the same increase as the overall index -- including professional salaries (58 percent), contracted services (54 percent), and books and periodicals (60 percent). Categories that have grown more slowly than the overall average increase in HEPI include supplies and materials (23 percent), equipment (33 percent), and utilities (32 percent).[2]

As Table 2 and Chart 2 indicate, the HEPI has not moved consistently over time with the Consumer Price Index (CPI). In the 1980s, increases in the HEPI generally were much greater than the growth of the CPI. Whereas the HEPI grew at 7 percent per year from 1980 to 1987, the CPI increased at a 5 percent annual compound growth rate. From 1975 to 1980, however, the CPI grew faster than the HEPI, increasing at nearly 9 percent per year while the HEPI rose 7.5 percent annually. In the early 1970s, the two indexes grew at roughly the same rate. In the 1960s, the HEPI grew nearly twice as fast as the CPI--5 percent annual growth in HEPI compared with less than 3 percent growth per year in the CPI. Cumulatively since 1961, the HEPI has grown one percentage point per year faster than the CPI, 6.3 percent for HEPI compared with an annual growth rate of 5.3 percent for the CPI.

The relatively high labor intensity of higher education is the principal reason why the HEPI and CPI have increased at different rates over time. Because personnel compensation represents such a large proportion of the HEPI, when compensation for faculty and other personnel lagged behind inflation in the late 1970s, the HEPI tended to increase more slowly than the CPI. Similarly, the increase above inflation in the salaries paid by colleges in the 1980s has contributed to the faster growth of the HEPI relative to the CPI in recent years.

The difference in the weights used to create these two indexes is another reason the HEPI and the CPI have not increased at the same rate over time. For example, utilities receive a lower weight in the HEPI than in the CPI because they represent a smaller proportion of the budgets of colleges and universities than they do in the budget of the average consumer. Thus, in the late 1970s, when utilities costs were skyrocketing, the HEPI grew more slowly than the CPI.[3]

The important point here is that if the increased prices of the goods and services that colleges purchase were the sole reason for increasing tuitions and other charges, we would expect to see college charges increasing at roughly the same rate as the HEPI. In the 1980s, the annual change in college tuitions thus would have been roughly two percentage points higher than the growth in the

TABLE 2

INCREASES IN THE HIGHER EDUCATION PRICE INDEX (HEPI) AND THE CONSUMER PRICE INDEX (CPI), 1961 TO 1987

	Average Annual Change (%)		Cumulative Change (%)	
	HEPI	CPI	HEPI	CPI
1961-65	3.9	1.3	16.4	5.5
1965-70	6.0	4.2	33.7	23.1
1970-75	6.6	6.7	37.4	38.6
1975-80	7.5	8.9	43.4	53.1
1980-87	6.8	4.7	58.4	37.9
1961-70	5.0	2.9	55.6	29.8
1970-80	7.0	7.8	97.1	112.2
1970-87	6.9	6.5	212.3	192.7
1961-87	6.3	5.3	386.1	279.9

SOURCES: HEPI: Research Associates of Washington, Higher Education Prices and Price Indexes, various years.
            CPI: U.S. Department of Labor, Bureau of Labor Statistics.

CHART 2
ANNUAL PERCENTAGE CHANGES IN THE HIGHER EDUCATION PRICE INDEX
(HEPI) AND THE CONSUMER PRICE INDEX (CPI), 1962 TO 1987

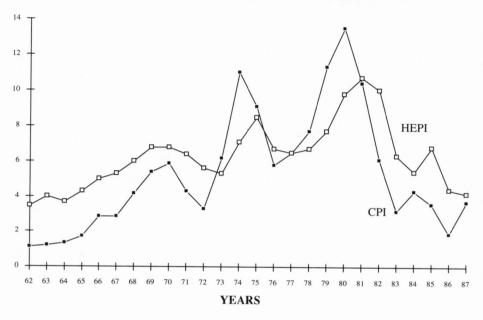

YEARS

CPI--mirroring the difference between HEPI and the CPI--rather than the five-point differential that has occurred in the 1980s.

The fact that the HEPI has increased faster than the CPI suggests that the rising cost of what colleges purchase has been an important force behind the recent steep rise in tuitions and other charges. But because the increase in HEPI falls considerably short of the growth in college charges, apparently other factors also have been at work. Without some other change in expenditure patterns or a contraction in revenue sources, the higher prices that colleges and universities face for what they purchase would not have pushed up tuitions as rapidly as they have risen.

As we have noted, because of data and conceptual limitations, the HEPI is not universally accepted as an accurate gauge of the prices that colleges and universities face. Therefore, it cannot be relied on as definitive in showing the degree to which increased cost pressures explain the increase in what colleges are charging their students. Many institutional officials, for example, report that the prices they pay for a wide variety of goods and services are increasing at an alarming rate. The culprits most frequently cited in the 1980s include laboratory equipment and facilities, library periodicals and books, and employee compensation. In the 1970s, utilities often were blamed.

The HEPI, however, is supposed to reflect the effects of these high-increase items. To the extent that the HEPI appears to be at odds with reports from institutional officials, at least two explanations may apply. First, although the items for which prices are increasing the fastest are included in the HEPI, they may receive relatively low weights compared with employee compensation and, therefore, may have relatively little impact on the overall increase in the HEPI. Second, the price structures of institutions vary because of many factors, including geographic location, size, relative commitment to research, and age of the institution and its physical plant. Officials of one institution may be correct when they cite skyrocketing prices for a particular good or service as the reason for their increasing charges, but the HEPI data suggests that this explanation is less valid for all colleges and universities nationwide.

A further look at the faculty issue. As we have indicated, the largest cost item for most colleges (and, as a result, the largest component of the HEPI) is the salaries and fringe benefits of faculty and other professional staff. The relatively high labor intensiveness of higher education and the real growth in faculty salaries in the 1980s are frequently cited by colleges and universities as major reasons their costs and charges have been increasing so fast in recent years. It appears that faculty salaries have been increasing more rapidly than inflation but less quickly than tuition in the 1980s. This recent trend is in contrast to the 1970s, when faculty salaries lagged behind both tuition increases and the general rate of inflation. [4]

The average change in faculty salaries for all ranks combined was roughly 7 percent per year from 1980 to 1987. (The percentage change in faculty salaries, therefore, is approximately the same as the change in the HEPI over this period, which should come as no surprise because faculty salaries are the largest single component of the HEPI.) But even with this recent growth, faculty salaries, adjusted for inflation, are not as high today as they were throughout most of the 1970s. As Chart 3 indicates, although salary levels for all professorial ranks increased in real terms through most of the 1980s, they are still lower in constant dollars than the salaries paid in the early 1970s.

CHART 3
TRENDS IN AVERAGE FACULTY SALARIES,
BY ACADEMIC RANK, 1971 TO 1987

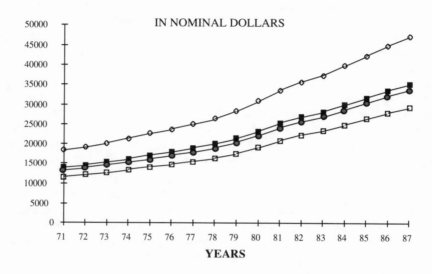

IN NOMINAL DOLLARS

YEARS

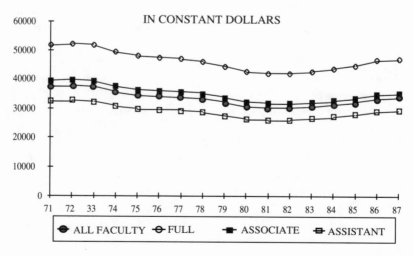

IN CONSTANT DOLLARS

Increases in faculty compensation, however, do not appear to be the principal reason for the increase in college tuitions in the 1980s. The growth in faculty salaries, like the HEPI generally, has been substantially slower than the increase in tuitions, as Chart 4 indicates. With the exception of 1973 and 1974, increases in faculty salaries have lagged behind annual tuition increases in every year since 1971, when data from the current time series on faculty salary growth were first collected. Even in the 1980s, when faculty salaries grew faster than the CPI, the increases were not as large as the increases in tuition in percentage terms. This surely has been a source of great irritation to faculty members at institutions where increases in tuition have not been reflected in similar increases in faculty salaries. Tuition increases of 10 percent do not sit well with faculty and other personnel who are receiving 5 or 6 percent salary increases.

Juxtaposing salary and tuition increases on the same chart naturally raises the issue: What is the relationship between the two? Did salary increases force institutions to raise their tuitions? Or did the growth in tuition revenues permit higher salary increases? Most probably, the answer is a combination of both. Increased competition with industry for scientists and engineers has created a labor market situation that drives up the salaries necessary to attract faculty in these fields. These cost pressures seemed to have become an integral part of the tuition-setting process in the 1980s. By the same token, the decision of institutional administrators to raise their tuitions creates revenues that can be used to increase faculty salaries in many fields, including the humanities and social sciences, where labor market conditions would not suggest the need for higher salaries.

On this point, it is worth asking the question of administrators: Why did faculty salaries in the 1980s increase faster than inflation in fields such as history, where the labor market is not appreciably better than it was in the 1970s, when salary increases lagged behind inflation? Part of the answer should be that higher real levels of tuition in the 1980s provided budgetary flexibility that did not exist in the 1970s, when tuitions did not keep pace with inflation.

Any discussion of faculty salaries also should include a caveat regarding the enormous variation in what faculty are paid at different institutions and in different fields of study. In 1987-88, the average salary for a professor of engineering or business and management exceeded $50,000, whereas the average for a professor in letters or the fine arts was $40,000. Average salaries at public institutions appear to be slightly higher than in the private sector. Faculty at major research universities generally receive larger salaries than those at other institutions. [5]

CHART 4
ANNUAL PERCENTAGE INCREASES
IN FACULTY SALARIES, THE CPI,
AND COLLEGE CHARGES, 1972 TO 1987

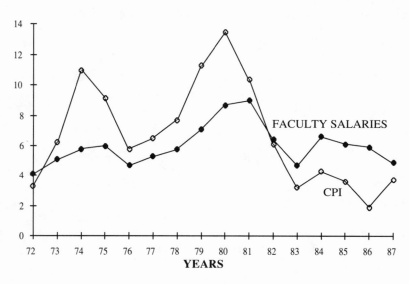

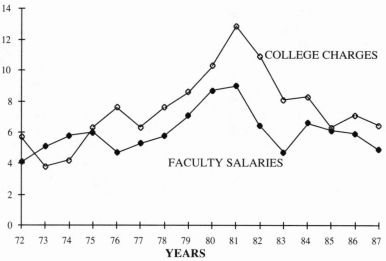

In many high-demand fields in the sciences, engineering, or business, where competition with industry is keen, the salaries paid to faculty are relatively generous, especially considering that these salaries are for nine or ten months and are frequently supplemented by summer school teaching or consulting. In high-demand fields at prestigious institutions, it is not unusual for today's faculty to receive six-digit salaries (not including the consulting or other fees they collect).

In presenting overall data on faculty salaries, both the American Association of University Professors (AAUP) and the Department of Education balance these relatively high salaries with the lower ones paid to faculty members at nonresearch institutions and in lower-demand fields such as the arts and humanities. In these areas, in many cases, faculty pay remains below that of other professions that many would regard as less prestigious. It is not uncommon, for example, for community college faculty to receive less compensation than teachers in the local school district. The growing disparity of faculty salaries is an issue that has substantial consequences for the future of the professoriate.

It is also the case that the growth in faculty salaries will not necessarily be the same as the growth in instructional costs. One reason is that instructional costs include items other than faculty compensation, such as the stipends paid to teaching assistants as well as the costs of equipment and materials. A more significant reason for a possible difference between increases in faculty salaries and instructional costs lies in the changing utilization of faculty at many institutions. These changes might involve the use of more part-time, adjunct faculty; the effects of retirement patterns and other supply conditions on the pay structure of the professoriate; or trends in faculty productivity.

The growing use of part-time instructional staff at many institutions, especially at community colleges and in continuing education programs, is one reason the growth of faculty salaries and instructional costs diverge over time. Between 1972 and 1983, the number of part-time instructors at four-year institutions grew by two-thirds, whereas the number of full-time faculty increased by only one-fifth. During that same time, the number of part-time instructors at two-year institutions nearly tripled, but the number of full-time faculty grew by less than one-third.[6] Comparable statistics are not available for the period since 1983, but overall faculty data suggest that the trend toward the use of part-time faculty members has continued on many campuses as a means for cutting costs and introducing additional flexibility in matching the demand for and supply of faculty. Substitution of part-time for full-time faculty would contribute to a situation in which faculty salary levels increased faster than instructional costs.

The changing age distribution of faculty members also helps to explain why faculty salaries and instructional costs can grow at different rates. As the large numbers of faculty who were hired in the 1950s and 1960s have grown older, the average age of the professoriate has increased. [7] This increase in the average age would suggest that faculty costs have grown over time because older faculty members typically receive higher salaries than younger faculty of equivalent rank. But as older faculty members retire and are replaced with younger faculty who command lower salaries, the costs of paying faculty could decline even though the salary of each active faculty member is increasing.

This condition would apply, however, only when the number of faculty members who are retiring is increasing relative to the total size of the faculty. Because no precise figures exist on the pattern of faculty retirements, it is difficult to estimate for the 1980s whether the aging of the professoriate or the increase in retirements had a larger impact on the growth in instructional costs. It seems reasonable to assume, however, that the dampening effect on costs of increased retirements will outweigh the higher salaries paid to older faculty members in the 1990s and into the first decades of the next century, as increasing numbers of faculty hired in the expansion periods of 1950s and 1960s retire.

This downward pressure on instructional costs, however, could be offset if the future supply of faculty is insufficient to meet the projected demand. In some scientific and engineering fields there is already a shortage of adequately trained faculty, and those shortages are likely to worsen. There also have been expressions of concern about the future labor market for faculty in many nonscientific fields, in which projected increases in enrollments beginning in the late 1990s, combined with accelerated faculty retirements and declining numbers of new doctorates, could lead to additional labor market shortages. If these shortages do materialize, cost pressures will intensify, and faculty salaries could increase accordingly.

Changes in faculty instructional "productivity" over time--such as increased ratios of students to faculty--could help explain why faculty salaries increase at a different rate from instructional costs. If higher expenditures per faculty member are being spread over larger numbers of students, then salaries could well be increasing faster than instructional costs per student. Available statistics on undergraduate enrollments and the number of full-time faculty, however, does not suggest that the ratio of students to faculty is increasing. If anything, it appears to be declining modestly. William Bowen and Julie Ann Sosa, in their analysis of faculty trends in the arts and sciences, indicate that the student/faculty ratio fell from 14.0/1 in 1977 to 10.3/1 in 1987.[8] Although there are many legitimate concerns about the precision of these data, and the declines could be a function of many factors, it still does not appear that student/faculty ratios are markedly on the increase.

Growth in instructional costs could be restrained further through other measures, such as greater emphasis on teaching skills relative to research achievements in faculty tenure and contract decisions; increases in teaching load; and greater use of emerging technologies in the teaching process. It appears that each of these possible teaching productivity enhancement measures has been underutilized on most campuses. Faculty tenure decisions remain biased toward research accomplishments, despite the growing call for better college-level teaching. Anecdotal reports suggest that the teaching loads of faculty members have been reduced over the past several decades, at least at many research-oriented universities. And although most colleges and universities have invested enormously in computers for their students, there is less evidence that new technologies have been sufficiently introduced into the teaching process. But while criticisms along these lines are probably justified, wholesale policy reversals could be damaging. For example, the rapid introduction of new technologies without adequate testing could well lead to declines in the quality of education provided.

"INCREASED TUITIONS ARE PAYING FOR EXPANDED SERVICES"

The preceding section examined the extent to which increases in the prices colleges pay for the goods and services they purchase explain the growth in college tuitions. A related but distinct issue is whether increases in the *quantity* of what colleges are purchasing, regardless of price, reasonably can be tied to increases in tuition and other charges. Defenders of the higher tuitions have argued that they are being used to pay for improving academic programs and for enhancing the level and content of important nonacademic services that colleges are providing to their students. Such activities include establishing new academic programs; recruiting and retaining good faculty; catching up on deferred maintenance; and providing more support services such as career placement, financial aid staff, and student counseling. Critics claim that instead of enhancing teaching and important services, too much of the increased revenues from higher tuitions are being spent on research and on unneeded services for students, additional administrative staff, and higher salaries. Who is right?

One means for investigating this issue is to examine how fast spending is increasing overall, and which categories of spending are increasing the fastest. More specifically, how fast is spending increasing? Which expenditure categories have increased the fastest? How much do spending patterns vary by type of institution?

For this analysis, we used the current funds expenditure data reported by colleges and universities through the Higher Education General Information Survey (HEGIS) from 1975-76 to 1985-86, the last year for which data were available when we conducted this analysis. There are a number of legitimate concerns associated with using this data source, including the capability of institutions to distinguish for reporting purposes between particular financial functions, questions about how resources are allocated among different campuses and central administration, the inherent fungibility of certain budget items, and the absence of capital expenditures from the current funds data base. To the extent that the survey methodology did not change materially for the period we are investigating, however, there is some assurance that examining trends over time in the HEGIS data should net some reasonable results, even if the spending levels defining those trends may be questionable.

Increases in overall expenditures. Total expenditures by all colleges and universities increased by 150 percent between 1975-76 and 1985-86, a compound annual rate of 9.6 percent. When calculated on a per-student basis, spending per full-time-equivalent (FTE) student increased between 1975 and 1985 by more than 140 percent, an average annual increase of 9.2 percent, as shown in Table 3. In the second half of the 1970s, expenditures by colleges grew by more than 60 percent, a compound annual growth rate of 10 percent, whereas in the first half of the 1980s, expenditures grew by 50 percent, an average compound growth rate of more than 8 percent.

The measure of inflation that is used to reflect the effects of inflation can make a substantial difference in how the real changes in these expenditure figures are presented. The two obvious measures of inflation are the Higher Education Price Index (HEPI) and the general rate of inflation, the Consumer Price Index (CPI). For the reasons discussed in the preceding section, the HEPI and the CPI have increased at different rates over the past several decades. For the 1980s, when the HEPI increased much faster than the CPI, using the HEPI to adjust for inflation will result in a lower real level of spending than will using the CPI.

TABLE 3
INCREASE IN TOTAL EXPENDITURES, ADJUSTED FOR DIFFERENT MEASURES OF INFLATION, 1975-76 TO 1985-86

	% Change 1975-76 to 1980-81			% Change 1980-81 to 1985-86			% Change 1975-76 to 1985-86		
	Current Dollars	Constant '85/HEPI	Constant '85/CPI	Current Dollars	Constant '85/HEPI	Constant '85/CPI	Current Dollars	Constant '85/HEPI	Constant '85/CPI
Public Institutions									
Expenditures									
Cumulative Change	61.5	12.6	5.5	49.5	2.5	14.5	141.3	15.4	20.7
Average Annual Change	10.1	2.4	1.1	8.4	0.5	2.7	9.2	1.4	1.9
Expenditures/FTE Student									
Cumulative Change	59.7	11.4	4.3	47.8	1.4	13.2	136.1	12.9	18.1
Average Annual Change	9.8	2.2	0.8	8.1	0.3	2.5	9.0	1.2	1.7
Private Institutions									
Expenditures									
Cumulative Change	71.2	19.3	11.8	57.7	8.2	20.8	170.0	29.1	35.1
Average Annual Change	11.3	3.6	2.3	9.5	1.6	3.9	10.4	2.6	3.1
Expenditures/FTE Student									
Cumulative Change	57.0	9.4	2.5	55.5	6.7	19.1	144.1	16.7	22.1
Average Annual Change	9.4	1.8	0.5	9.2	1.3	3.6	9.3	1.6	2.0
All Institutions									
Expenditures									
Cumulative Change	64.6	14.8	7.5	52.3	4.5	16.6	150.7	19.9	25.4
Average Annual Change	10.5	2.8	1.5	8.8	0.9	3.1	9.6	1.8	2.3
Expenditures/FTE Student									
Cumulative Change	61.0	12.3	5.2	50.5	3.3	15.3	142.4	15.9	21.3
Average Annual Change	10.0	2.3	1.0	8.5	0.6	2.9	9.3	1.5	1.9

SOURCE: U.S. Department of Education, *Digest of Education Statistics*, 1988.

When adjusted for the HEPI, expenditures per student at all institutions increased by 4.5 percent between 1980 and 1985, or by less than 1 percent per year. If the CPI is used as the adjustment factor, however, the real increase in expenditures between 1980 and 1985 was 16.6 percent, or 3 percent per year (see Table 3). The differences that result from using the HEPI and the CPI as the inflation adjustment factor in turn can lead to disagreements over how fast college spending is increasing. Chester Finn, former assistant secretary of education, for example, argued that "the unit costs have indisputably risen, even as the enterprise has grown. (Conventional economic theory has it that expansion ordinarily brings certain economies of scale.) In 1986-87, the average expenditure from 'education and general' funds per full-time-equivalent student was $8,924 on American campuses. This was 3 percent more--in real terms--than in the previous year, 17 percent more than three years before, and 24 percent more than in 1981-82." [9]

Finn's assertiveness about the increase in costs is misleading, however. First, the number of students enrolled in higher education has not increased substantially over the past decade. Instead, enrollments have remained relatively level, increasing on average 1 percent per year, a far cry from the rapid growth of the 1960s. The inability to spread fixed costs over a growing number of students may have contributed greatly to rising costs per student, as is discussed later in this section.

Second, much of Finn's argument is premised on using the CPI as the measure against which expenditures should be judged. This is disingenuous, given that the department's own publications, such as the *Digest of Education Statistics*, regularly use the HEPI to adjust college expenditures for the effects of inflation. Finn's use of the CPI to make the point about the growth of spending is reminiscent of the actions of other education pundits who chose to use the CPI as the adjustment for inflation, when it exceeded the growth in HEPI in the 1970s--making the real growth in expenditures seem smaller--and who then switched back to using the HEPI in the 1980s, when it helps to moderate the reported growth in inflation-adjusted spending.

Obviously this issue is as much political as it is analytic. Arguments can be mustered on either side. The HEPI was developed precisely to address the issue of what it costs colleges to do business, and therefore it would seem more appropriate as a measure of the inflation that colleges and universities face. On the other hand, the HEPI is to a large extent internally generated through its heavy weighting of personnel costs, and a reasonable argument can be made that the CPI should be used as the adjustment factor, because it is what is used for most real dollar calculations in other circumstances. On balance, it seems to us more appropriate to use the HEPI to adjust college expenditures for inflation but to use the CPI to view the issue from the student's or consumer's perspective on real changes in the price of a college education.

The impact of enrollment trends on spending. Table 3 also indicates that in the late 1970s and early 1980s, the difference between total and per-student spending increases was very small, with one exception: In the private sector during the late 1970s, the increase in per-student expenditures was two percentage points per year less than spending measured on an aggregate basis. The general closeness in the growth of total and per-student spending since the mid-1970s is in distinct contrast to the patterns of earlier decades. This changing relationship between total and per-student spending correlates directly with changing enrollment patterns, which suggests that enrollments may be helpful in explaining the growth of spending over time.

Beginning in the 1950s and extending into the first half of the 1970s, enrollments at American colleges and universities grew rapidly. Enrollments increased by one-half in the 1950s, more than doubled in the 1960s, and grew by about one-third in the first half of the 1970s. With this expansion, many institutional administrators may have gotten accustomed to the notion that they could increase their rates of total spending faster than their expenditures per student by allowing growth in the number of students enrolled to absorb much of the shock from higher expenditure levels. Faculties and facilities increased as well, but at most institutions the overall growth in resources was not as great as the increase in enrollments. The result was that per-student spending did not increase nearly as fast as total expenditures.

In the first half of the 1960s higher education expenditures more than tripled, increasing at an annual average rate of 14 percent, as shown in Chart 5. In contrast, spending per student during this time increased at an average rate of less than 5 percent per year. This pattern continued in the second half of the 1960s, as total expenditures increased 12 percent per year while per-student spending grew by 3 percent per year. Similarly, in the first half of the 1970s, when total spending increased nearly 12 percent per year, per-student expenditures increased at an annual compound rate of less than 7 percent.

The patterns in the 1960s and early 1970s are substantially different from the experience since 1975, however. Between 1975 and 1980, aggregate spending grew at an annual rate of slightly more than 10 percent, and spending per student increased slightly less than 10 percent. From 1980 to 1985, total expenditures and spending per student increased at roughly the same rate of between 8 and 9 percent for aggregate and per-student expenditures.

CHART 5
AVERAGE ANNUAL PERCENTAGE GROWTH
IN TOTAL AND PER-STUDENT EXPENDITURES,
BY CONTROL OF INSTITUTION, 1955 TO 1985

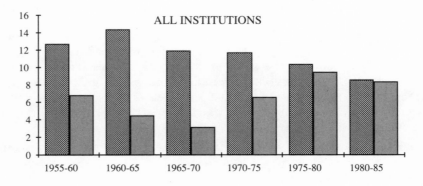

ALL INSTITUTIONS

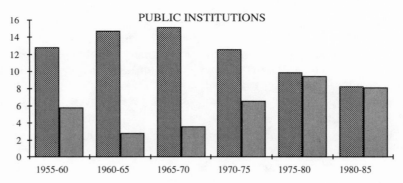

PUBLIC INSTITUTIONS

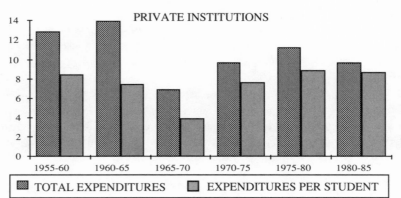

PRIVATE INSTITUTIONS

TOTAL EXPENDITURES   EXPENDITURES PER STUDENT

It seems reasonable to argue that the growth of enrollments in earlier decades allowed many institutions the luxury of increasing their spending without imposing severe price hikes. The spreading of fixed costs over larger numbers of students that is inherent in expansion allowed institutions to increase their budgets without feeling the effects in the form of similarly higher expenditures per student. This benefit of expansion can be derived as long as the growth in enrollments does not require increases in capital and other expenditures, thus raising the average costs per student. It can be passed along to the student consumer in the form of less steep price increases, albeit with fewer resources per student. This pricing luxury has not been available since the mid-1970s, however, when enrollments began to level.

Enrollment increases at public institutions were especially rapid in the 1960s and into the early 1970s--many schools expanded as fast as their state legislatures would allow. Total public sector enrollments grew by 80 percent in the 1960s and by another 40 percent in the first half of the 1970s before they started to level. Public campus administrators were thus able to ride a curve of growing enrollments, as formulas tied to enrollment levels stimulated larger state appropriations. These campuses also benefited from the fact that the funding they received generally was based on the average cost per student. To the extent that the additional state revenues generated from growing enrollments typically exceeded the additional costs associated with educating those new students, many public institutions enjoyed a revenue windfall.

These funding formulas, however, can have a debilitating effect when enrollments stop growing and start declining, as long as average costs continue to exceed marginal costs. In such situations, the decrease in funding will exceed an institution's ability to cut its costs, placing severe pressure on institutional budgets. This dilemma is the source of a fundamental axiom of college budgeting: Managing an institution when enrollments are level or declining is far more difficult than when enrollments are expanding.

In the private sector, enrollments grew less rapidly than in the public sector during the 1960s and 1970s, and private institutions did not have the enticement of state enrollment-based funding to spur their search for students. Nonetheless, total private sector enrollments did grow by about 40 percent in the 1960s before they slowed in the 1970s, and there were plenty of examples of expanding institutions.

One prevalent form of private sector growth during this time was at traditionally single-sex colleges that became coeducational. At Williams College, for example, enrollments jumped when the college went coeducational in 1970, a growth not initially matched by an increase in resources. As a result, expenditures per student increased less than total spending in the early 1970s, and tuitions rose at a relatively modest rate. In the mid-1970s, however, Williams apparently decided that it had not increased its resources sufficiently to maintain its quality, and the college then increased its spending much more rapidly. Because the number of students at Williams rose only marginally from the mid-1970s to the mid-1980s, the surge in expenditures was not mitigated by being spread across a larger student population. Spending per student grew by more than $3,100 in constant dollars from 1975-76 to 1985-86, and tuitions grew rapidly as well.[10]

The possibility that enrollment growth in the private sector has helped to restrain the growth in per-student expenditures and prices is not limited to single-sex institutions that became coeducational. Jack Dunn and Dawn Terkla, researchers at Tufts University, have speculated on this issue as it relates to their institution.[11] After going through a list of nine of the various reasons that are traditionally given for why college costs have increased, they suggest a tenth factor when they comment, "We stopped growing." They go on to explain why they believe that stable enrollments could have that impact on institutional finances, especially in limiting new revenues. Dunn and Terkla caution that their speculations may not be broadly applicable to other institutions, and they encourage researchers at other colleges and universities to examine the data at their own institutions. From our examination of the national data, we believe that the linkage between enrollment patterns and cost/tuition increases may be applicable to a wide range of institutions in both the private and public sectors.

Chart 5 also demonstrates that differences in the growth of aggregate and per-student expenditures have narrowed greatly over time in both the public and private sectors as enrollment growth has slowed. At public institutions, enrollment growth was much larger in the 1960s and early 1970s than the growth experienced by the private sector. Therefore, the difference between aggregate and per-student spending during this time was greater at public institutions. The narrowing in the difference between aggregate and per-student spending beginning in the late 1970s was thus more dramatic at public institutions.

But the private sector also experienced enrollment growth in the 1960s and into the early 1970s, which led to large differences between its aggregate and per student spending growth. For example, in the first half of the 1960s, public sector expenditures grew by 15 percent per year, whereas annual per-student spending increased by less than 3 percent. During that same time, private sector expenditures increased by 14 percent per year, whereas annual per-student spending grew by less than 8 percent. In the late 1970s and early 1980s, however, the difference between total and per-student spending was greater in the private sector, indicating that its enrollments were then growing faster than in the public sector.

The growth in expenditure categories. Instructional costs for faculty salaries and related teaching activities are the largest component of college expenditures in the statistics reported by the Department of Education. They also were the largest source of increased expenditures, as Table 4 indicates. Between 1975-76 and 1985-86, they accounted for two-fifths of the increase in Education and General (E & G) expenditures at public institutions and one-third of the increase at private institutions. One possible reason for this growth in instructional costs may have been curriculum shifts from liberal arts courses toward more expensive science, engineering, and business administration programs, which reflected shifts in enrollments. As we have previously noted, however, the growth in instructional costs may have been restrained by the increased use of part-time faculty and by productivity enhancements. The next largest increase between 1975 and 1985 among the (E&G) spending categories was administration, which represented about one-fifth of the expenditure increase in both the public and private sectors.

As indicated in Chart 6, the percentage increase in each of the expenditure categories except libraries and mandatory transfers exceeded the increase in the CPI and the HEPI between 1975 and 1980. All categories except operations and maintenance grew faster than the CPI and the HEPI from 1980 to 1985. (The relatively slow growth in operations and maintenance probably is a function of lower utilities costs in the 1980s and decisions to defer maintenance needs.)

But the categories with the largest percentage increases in the late 1970s differed from those in the first half of the 1980s. Between 1975 and 1980, the largest percentage increases in expenditures in both the public and private sectors were for administration, student services, and operations and maintenance (which was a function of the soaring utilities costs in the 1970s; see Table 4). Public service activities and research also generated large percentage increases in the latter 1970s, particularly in the public sector. In the first half of the 1980s, however, the largest percentage increases in expenditures were for administration in both public and private institutions, and in student services, student aid, and public service activities at private institutions.

Despite these differences in growth patterns, however, spending in various categories as a proportion of total expenditures changed relatively little over the period from 1975 to 1985, as Table 4 clearly shows. Instructional costs as a

TABLE 4

TRENDS IN HIGHER EDUCATION EXPENDITURE CATEGORIES, 1975-76 TO 1985-86

PUBLIC INSTITUTIONS

	Current $, in Millions			% of Total Expenditures			Dollar Difference, in Millions			% Change, in Current $		
	1975-76	1980-81	1985-86	1975-76	1980-81	1985-86	1975-80	1980-85	1975-85	1975-80	1980-85	1975-85
Instruction	9516	14850	21881	36.3	35.1	34.6	5334	7031	12365	56.1	47.3	129.9
Administr.	3305	5405	8676	12.6	12.8	13.7	2100	3271	5371	63.5	60.5	162.5
Student Serv.	1115	1951	2922	4.3	4.6	4.6	836	971	1807	75.0	49.8	162.1
Research	2154	3813	5705	8.2	9.0	9.0	1659	1892	3551	77.0	49.6	164.9
Libraries	825	1187	1685	3.2	2.8	2.7	362	498	860	43.9	42.0	104.2
Public Service	1036	1719	2516	4.0	4.1	4.0	683	797	1480	65.9	46.4	142.9
Oper. & Maint.	2158	3682	5177	8.2	8.7	8.2	1524	1495	3019	70.6	40.6	139.9
Transfers	375	501	736	1.4	1.2	1.2	126	235	361	33.6	46.9	96.3
Student Aid	799	1065	1576	3.1	2.5	2.5	266	511	777	33.3	48.0	97.2
Total E&G Expenditures	21283	34173	50874	81.3	80.8	80.5	12890	16701	29591	60.6	48.9	139.0
Non E&G Expenditures	4901	8106	12321	18.7	19.2	19.5	3205	4215	7420	65.4	52.0	151.4
Total Expenditures	26184	42279	63195	100.0	100.0	100.0	16095	20916	37011	61.5	49.5	141.3

TABLE 4 (Continued)

TRENDS IN HIGHER EDUCATION EXPENDITURE CATEGORIES, 1975-76 TO 1985-86

PRIVATE INSTITUTIONS

	Current $, in Millions			% of Total Expenditures			Dollar Difference, in Millions			% Change, in Current $		
	1975-76	1980-81	1985-86	1975-76	1980-81	1985-86	1975-80	1980-85	1975-85	1975-80	1980-85	1975-85
Instruction	3579	5883	9151	28.1	27.0	26.6	2304	3268	5572	64.4	55.5	155.7
Administr.	1559	2880	4792	12.3	13.2	14.0	1321	1912	3233	84.7	66.4	207.4
Student Serv.	510	958	1641	4.0	4.4	4.8	448	683	1131	87.8	71.3	221.8
Research	1133	1844	2732	8.9	8.5	8.0	711	888	1599	62.8	48.2	141.1
Libraries	399	573	866	3.1	2.6	2.5	174	293	467	43.6	51.1	117.0
Public Serv.	203	339	604	1.6	1.6	1.8	136	265	401	67.0	78.2	197.5
Oper. & Maint.	925	1668	2428	7.3	7.7	7.1	743	760	1503	80.3	45.6	162.5
Transfers	171	314	457	1.3	1.4	1.3	143	143	286	83.6	45.5	167.3
Student Aid	837	1440	2584	6.6	6.6	7.5	603	1144	1747	72.0	79.4	208.7
Total E&G Expenditures	9316	15899	25255	73.2	73.0	73.5	6583	9356	15939	70.7	58.8	171.1
Non E&G Expenditures	3404	5872	9086	26.8	27.0	26.5	2468	3214	5682	72.5	54.7	166.9
Total Expenditures	12720	21771	34341	100.0	100.0	100.0	9051	12570	21621	71.2	57.7	170.0

NOTES: "Non E&G Expenditures" includes Auxiliary Enterprises, Hospitals, and Independent Operations. "Total Expenditures" is elsewhere referred to as Current Fund sExpenditures.

SOURCE: U.S. Department of Education, *Digest of Education Statistics*, 1988.

CHART 6
PERCENTAGE INCREASE IN EDUCATION
AND GENERAL EXPENDITURE CATEGORIES,
1975 TO 1980 AND 1980 TO 1985

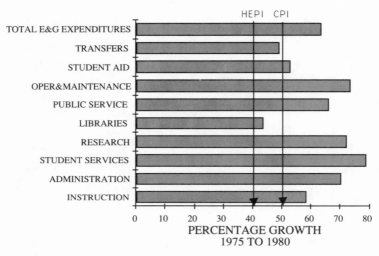

PERCENTAGE GROWTH
1975 TO 1980

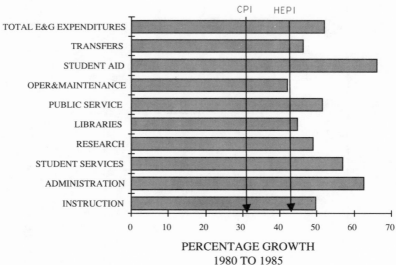

PERCENTAGE GROWTH
1980 TO 1985

proportion of total expenditures decreased by about one percentage point between 1975 and 1985, whereas administrative costs increased by about one percentage point. All of the other categories maintained roughly the same share of spending in 1985 as was the case in 1975. Even the rapid growth in student aid at private institutions in the first half of the 1980s raised its proportion of total expenditures by only one percentage point. (This confirms the arithmetic fact that large increases in a relatively small category typically do not result in a large increase in its overall share of the pie.)

Expenditure patterns by type of institution. The growth of total expenditures between 1975 and 1985 was fairly similar for public and private institutions. Spending at public institutions grew by 140 percent from 1975 to 1985, an average annual increase of 9.2 percent. For private institutions, expenditures grew by 170 percent, an average annual growth rate of more than 10 percent. In the first half of the 1980s, the difference in expenditure growth between public and private institutions shrank, as spending increased by 50 percent at public institutions and 58 percent at private institutions. Moreover, much of this difference in spending growth can be accounted for by the increase in student aid provided by private institutions. If expenditures were examined net of student aid-- that is, if student aid was treated more as a discount from revenues than as a real expenditure -- then there would be little difference in the expenditure growth patterns of public and private institutions in the 1980s.

The differences in how public and private institutions spend their funds are much smaller than the variations in their revenue sources. In 1985-86, instructional costs represented 43 percent of E&G expenditures of public institutions and 36 percent in the independent sector, as Table 5 indicates. For most other categories, the expenditure shares are very similar, with the exception of student aid and non-E&G expenditures, which constitute a larger share of the spending at private institutions.

Where large differences in expenditure patterns do exist is by type of institution within the public and independent sectors. Public two-year colleges devote half of their budgets to instructional costs, whereas the proportion at public universities is less than 40 percent. Much of this difference can be accounted for by the fact that two-year colleges spend virtually nothing on research, whereas one-fifth of public university E&G expenditures are for research activities. At all three types of private institutions, instructional costs constitute about one-third of all education and general expenditures. As in the public sector, research represents about one-fifth of expenditures at private

TABLE 5

PERCENT DISTRIBUTION OF E&G EXPENDITURES BY TYPE AND CONTROL OF INSTITUTION, 1985-86

	PUBLIC			
Expenditure Category	2-Year	4-Year	University	All
Instruction	49.9	45.0	37.7	43.0
Administration	20.7	18.4	13.9	17.1
Student Services	9.0	6.2	3.7	5.7
Research	0.1	8.2	19.7	11.2
Libraries	2.9	3.6	3.2	3.3
Public Service	2.0	3.3	8.0	4.9
Oper. & Maint.	11.9	10.7	8.8	10.2
Transfers	1.4	1.8	1.2	1.5
Student Aid	2.2	2.9	3.8	3.1
TOTAL	100.0	100.0	100.0	100.0

	PRIVATE			
Expenditure Category	2-Year	4-Year	University	All
Instruction	34.0	35.1	37.8	36.2
Administration	26.7	21.7	15.0	19.0
Student Services	12.1	8.3	3.8	6.5
Research	0.0	4.8	18.5	10.8
Libraries	2.7	3.5	3.5	3.4
Public Service	0.4	2.6	2.4	2.4
Oper. & Maint.	12.9	10.2	8.6	9.6
Transfers	2.0	2.3	1.3	1.8
Student Aid	9.2	11.5	9.1	10.2
TOTAL	100.0	100.0	100.0	100.0

NOTE: Details may not add to totals due to rounding.
SOURCE: U.S. Department of Education, *Digest of Education Statistics*, 1988.

universities, but less than one-tenth at the other four-year institutions, and no research expenditures are recorded at private two-year colleges.

Spending categories meriting additional analysis. The preceding overview of the data on expenditure trends indicates that several categories of expenditures merit special attention and further analysis, including the costs associated with administration, student services, and sponsored research, and the method of accounting for capital investments.

The growth in administrative costs. It is difficult to examine the data on college expenditures without becoming curious about what is happening in the area of administrative costs. In the late 1970s, the growth in administrative costs tracked with other expenditure trends. But in the first half of the 1980s, these costs surged upward, running counter to what one would expect during a period of level enrollments and even some retrenchment in higher education.

Department of Education officials in the Reagan administration, after examining the HEGIS financial data, concluded that administrative costs are a principal engine driving up college expenditures. In January 1988 the department issued a report intended to support this contention. The report noted that administrative expenditures grew from 18 cents of every dollar spent on instruction in 1960 to nearly 30 cents in 1985. (The report, however, virtually ignored the fact that in the past decade, despite the continued rapid growth of administrative costs, their percentage of *total* spending increased by only one percentage point.) The report further noted that over time, administrative staff had grown as a share of total staff. In addition to examining national expenditure and staffing trends, the report also contained a set of case studies providing more detailed data on administrative costs at selected institutions.[12]

The department's report on administrative costs helped to identify and elaborate on this interesting and important financial trend in higher education. In that respect, the department should be commended. But the report failed to answer a number of questions which must be examined before we can draw any reasonable conclusions about the trends in administrative costs. For example, what kinds of administrative expenditures increased? Was the increased spending for more central administrative staff or for specific student services, such as career counselors or financial aid officers? Was the increase in administrative costs used to pay higher salaries or to hire more staff?

An increase in expenditures for more positions or higher salaries in the "overhead" category would be hard to justify when enrollments have not markedly increased. But if the increased administrative expenditures were for expanded services--such as career placement or other support activities that students and their parents have requested--they may have been perfectly appropriate. Higher administrative costs also could be a function of increased marketing and recruitment costs, as institutions--especially in the private sector-- try to attract students from a diminishing pool of traditional college-age applicants.

Some observers have been critical of these augmented marketing efforts. But how reasonable is it for proponents of a "free market" system to advise college and university officials simply to throw up their hands and declare it unseemly to compete for students? In a similar vein, the department's report decried the fact that administrative costs appear to have increased fastest at private sector institutions. But if these costs have been devoted to expansion of development efforts, it is not reasonable for those who advocate reduced dependence on federal funds to belittle fund-raising intended to increase the amount of private resources available to colleges and universities.

Another possible source of higher administrative costs may be the increased burden of responding to governmental regulations and the costs of avoiding or responding to the threat of litigation. On the first point, many college officials contend that the costs of complying with federal and state regulations-- in areas such as health, safety, pollution, and financial accountability--are substantial and growing, and add greatly to staffing requirements. On the second point, colleges and universities have not been immune to society's growing tendency to settle disputes through litigation, and liability on campus for such things as crime prevention, drinking- and drug-related incidents, and equal rights enforcement adds to staff needs. To make these points stick, however, colleges must demonstrate not only that regulatory and legal requirements are burdensome, but that their impact has been heavier on college operations and budgets than on other sectors of society. They have not yet demonstrated this convincingly, however.[13]

It is also true that a subtle but major transformation has occurred at many colleges and universities over the past several decades, as they have sought to improve the efficiency of their operations. Many have hired more accountants, MBAs, and other professional staff and have increased their use of consultants to develop management information and accounting systems, to plan capital campaigns, to manage their real estate holdings, and to perform other functions. What once were haphazard and desultory campus activities now appear to be high-profile efforts, and critical to the operation of an institution. This shift reflects the growing complexity of running a modern college or university. To some extent, this transformation of academe into a more business-like operation may be what the statistics show as a dramatic increase in administrative costs.

In the context of this report, the question is whether the increase in administrative costs reasonably can be established as a primary cause of the increase in college charges. The HEGIS data would suggest that the answer is no. Despite the relatively large increase in the costs of administration, these costs did not grow appreciably as a percentage of total expenditures between 1980 and 1985 in either the public or private sectors. Therefore, it does not appear that administrative costs can be assigned a principal role in the debate over why college charges increased so fast in the 1980s.

To determine why administrative costs have been increasing at a relatively rapid rate, more research is needed. In this area, case studies can be particularly useful. Institutional finance and business officers would seem to be a reasonable group to undertake such a task. Such an examination should include not only an analysis of which types of administrative costs have grown the most but also a consideration of whether the additional resources devoted to achieve management efficiencies have achieved their stated purpose.

The growing availability of student support services. Another trend in American higher education in recent years has been the more extensive provision of a wide range of student support services. For example, most colleges today have a career placement office on campus, a service that was not nearly so available two or more decades ago. Similarly, much more is provided now in the way of personal counseling. Still another example is the expanded availability of tutoring and mentoring services and facilities for students. All of these contribute to the rapid growth in "student services" expenditures.

One reason why these expenditures have grown over time is that students and their families expect more of these services to be provided and appear willing to pay for them. Most institutions would not have decided to establish or expand these services without some instigation from their consumers. Although no solid data exist on this point, anecdotal evidence and reports from campuses suggest that these services have flourished because students want and need them.

Another reason expenditures for these kinds of services have grown may have to do with the changing demographics of American higher education. Over the past two decades, college students have become decidedly older and more likely to attend on a part-time basis. The fact that colleges and universities have reached out more to nontraditional student groups may have had some consequences for how these institutions finance themselves. Many administrators contend that older, nontraditional students generally require more remedial services, greater administrative support, and more counseling than do their full-time, traditional-age counterparts. If this is true, the growing number of older college students result in increasing costs to institutions.

The rising costs associated with sponsored research. Although teaching has been and remains the primary function of most American colleges and universities, it is not the only one. Conducting research and performing public service are two other important areas of responsibility. American research universities have established themselves over time as the best in the world. The large and growing numbers of foreign graduate students that enroll in these institutions attest to their continued worldwide reputation.

A variety of statistics confirm the growing importance of the research function on American campuses. More than half of all the basic research performed in this country is conducted on university campuses or by organizations with university affiliations. Although several other spending categories grew faster, research expenditures still grew in real terms from the mid-1970s through the mid-1980s. Contrary to public perceptions, federal support for campus research, which represents about 75 percent of all dollars spent for research conducted on campus, grew at an annual real rate of 4 percent per year in the 1980s. Nor was this growth in federal research support confined to the Department of Defense; domestic-based research grew nearly as fast as defense-related activities. Thus, research was one of the few areas of growth among domestic discretionary programs during the Reagan era. These statistics indicate that campus-based research continues to be strongly supported by both the federal government and the institutions themselves.

There is now some reason to believe that several related aspects of the research enterprise on campus may be contributing to the rapid growth of both overall college expenditures and tuitions. Despite the growth in real terms of federal support for campus research in the 1980s, many administrators believe that this growth has not been sufficient to keep up with the skyrocketing costs of conducting research. Salaries for scientific and engineering faculty and associated costs are also being driven up through stiffer competition with industry. Institutions are finding that they must also invest heavily in facilities, equipment, and support staff, in addition to direct salary and benefits, to attract a top-notch research scientist or engineer. Administrators also point out that the recovery of indirect costs from the federal government for many years has been insufficient to pay fully for the costs attached to doing sponsored research. And it appears that the impact of federal support has been diluted as more projects are being funded at lower average federal support per project.

The net result of these trends is that the growth in the real level of federal support for campus-based research is often insufficient to meet the full costs of each project. Many universities then feel obliged to use an increasing proportion of their own resources to fund research that is conducted on their campuses. Although an institution may be "losing" money with each new research grant it receives, the structure of the enterprise, including faculty pressures, makes it difficult to hold back in competing for new research grants. Moreover, to the extent that many research-related expenses are fixed, the only way to recoup these costs is to compete for additional grants and contracts. Still, the accumulated pressures of this system apparently are leading some university administrators to rethink their traditional commitment to place little or no rein on their faculty to compete for new research funding.

Nor are these research pressures entirely federally created. There are also the internal needs of faculty to publish and do research that may or may not correspond to federal priorities. In professions such as medicine, law, business, and engineering, certain levels of research may be required for institutions to meet the mandates of accrediting agencies. In deciding how to allocate scarce resources, administrators and faculty often face difficult choices in resolving the funding and time allocation tensions between the teaching and research functions.

Although good teaching and good research often reinforce one another, sometimes emphasizing one function tends to diminish the other. Reduced teaching loads and a heavy weighting on research publications in tenure and contract decisions can undermine the quality of teaching. If an institution decides to upgrade its reputation in research, that decision often affects the resources it can or is willing to devote to teaching. Similarly, of course, a college's commitment to the teaching of undergraduates may detract from a faculty member's time and ability to do research.

In this study we do not seek to judge whether the choices that institutions are making in arbitrating among competing pressures to teach and do research are proper. Each institution must address these issues in its own way. The point is that the choices an institution makes in this regard may be having an impact on the level of tuitions they charge. If the shortfall in the federal support of research is paid for directly or indirectly with tuition revenues, then the choice to support research will affect the price structure that undergraduates face. For many years undergraduate tuitions at many universities have supported research by paying for a substantial portion of the fellowships and assistantships that institutions provide to graduate students. But this traditional form of cross-subsidy now appears to have been extended to the use of undergraduate tuitions for the direct support of campus-based research.

The trade-offs that research universities make between research and teaching also may be having a more subtle impact on the price structure of all of higher education because these institutions typically act as price leaders in the higher education "industry." They are frequently the trendsetters to which other institutions look in deciding what price to charge their students. If research pressures are affecting the price and cost structure at research universities, then those pressures indirectly may be affecting what many nonresearch institutions charge their students as well. This notion of price leadership is discussed more fully in the section on competitive pressures and the tuition-setting process.

Accounting for capital expenditures. Many campus administrators believe that greater "capitalization" is one reason why costs have increased so much over the past decade. This increased investment in capital items can be seen on many campuses in the form of new computer centers, sophisticated laboratory equipment, and other impressive new facilities. We would expect to see this growing capital intensity reflected in the statistics on the value of physical plant per student, which increased from $9,866 in 1979-80 to $13,671 in 1985-86. Yet, when adjusted for inflation, these figures indicate that there was virtually no real growth in the value of the physical plant in the first half of the 1980s. [14]

This difference between perception and the existing statistical evidence reflects a recurrent data concern regarding capital expenditures by colleges and universities. Our discussion of expenditures in this study, for example, does not reflect the growth in capital outlays over time because Department of Education data on finances historically has differentiated between current funds and capital expenditures. Thus, the data on expenditures that are analyzed in this report, and that are used in virtually all other analyses of college costs, are the figures on current funds expenditures, which reflect only a relatively small portion of growth in capital outlays. For example, current funds expenditures generally include the purchase of microcomputers, but in most cases they do not include the costs associated with building a computer center on campus or the purchase of a supercomputer costing many millions of dollars. Construction and renovation of academic and dormitory facilities also generally do not appear as current funds expenditures, although if bonds were used to finance such a facility, the interest payments on the debt could very well appear as current funds expenditures in the form of "mandatory transfers."

This report is not the proper place to discuss the nuances of how the Department of Education or colleges and universities do their accounting. Yet it is important to recognize that the current funds expenditure item typically used in analyses of college costs does not reflect much of the campus activity subsumed under capital investment. If capital investment has increased over time, that growth will not be reflected in the spending figures used here. Given the campus-based reports on greater capitalization, additional data collection and more realistic analysis of capital spending trends are merited.

"NONTUITION REVENUE SOURCES ARE CONTRACTING"

As we have noted, tuitions and fees are far from the only source of revenues for colleges and universities. If nontuition revenue sources are not growing as fast as before, then colleges and universities may be forced to raise tuitions to maintain the levels of services they provide. Thus, a shortfall in other revenue sources could be a primary reason tuitions have been increasing so fast in the 1980s. In this section, we examine the trends in nontuition revenue sources in both the public and private sectors of higher education. What has been the pattern of increase for these revenue sources? To what extent has a slowdown in their growth pressured institutions to increase tuitions and fees?

Table 6 indicates the trends in major revenue categories between 1975-76 and 1985-86. Like the statistics on expenditures, the data for revenues come from the HEGIS, an imperfect source but one that does provide fairly consistent data on changes over time. As the table indicates, between 1975 and 1985 the share of revenues derived from different sources has changed moderately. Tuition and fees as a source of funds increased somewhat in both the public and private sectors. At public institutions, tuition and fees increased from 13.0 percent of total revenues in 1975 to 14.5 percent in 1985. For private institutions, tuition and fees grew from 36.5 percent of all revenues in 1975 to 38.6 percent in 1985.

Federal government funds dropped as a share of revenues in both the public and private sectors. Federal dollars as a proportion of all public revenues fell from over 13 percent in 1975 to less than 11 percent in 1985; for private institutions they decreased from 14 percent in 1975 to less than 11 percent in 1985. Most of the decrease in the federal share of revenues is attributable to the relatively level funding in the federal student aid that institutions have received; as a result, the share of institutional revenues related to student aid declined. Federal funds for sponsored research, on the other hand, maintained their share of total institutional revenues. (It is also worth noting that the rapid growth in the

TABLE 6
TRENDS IN HIGHER EDUCATION REVENUE SOURCES, 1975-76 TO 1985-86

	Current Dollars, in Millions			% of Total Revenues			Dollar Difference, in Millions			% Change, in Current $		
	1975-80	1980-81	1985-86	1975-76	1980-81	1985-86	1975-80	1980-85	1975-85	1975-80	1980-85	1975-85
Public Institutions												
Tuition and Fees	3478	5570	9439	13.0	12.9	14.5	2092	3869	5961	60.1	69.5	171.4
Federal Gov.	3603	5470	6821	13.4	12.7	10.5	1867	1351	3218	51.8	24.7	89.3
State Govs.	11963	19676	29221	44.6	45.6	44.9	7713	9545	17258	64.5	48.5	144.3
Local Govs.	1500	1623	2326	5.6	3.8	3.6	123	703	826	8.2	43.3	55.1
Priv. Gifts, etc.	616	1100	2110	2.3	2.5	3.2	484	1010	1494	78.6	91.8	242.5
Endowment Income	97	215	399	0.4	0.5	0.6	118	184	302	121.6	85.6	311.3
Educ. Activities	423	944	1597	1.6	2.2	2.5	521	653	1174	123.2	69.2	277.5
Indep. Operations	398	70	153	1.5	0.2	0.2	-328	83	-245	-82.4	118.6	-61.6
Other Sources	4757	8528	13060	17.7	19.7	20.1	3771	4532	8303	79.3	53.1	174.5
Total Revenues	26835	43196	65126	100.0	100.0	100.0	16361	21930	38291	61.0	50.8	142.7
Private Institutions												
Tuition and Fees	4694	8203	13677	36.5	36.6	38.6	3509	5474	8983	74.8	66.7	191.4
Federal Gov.	1811	3009	3751	14.1	13.4	10.6	1198	742	1940	66.2	24.7	107.1
State Govs.	297	430	691	2.3	1.9	2.0	133	261	394	44.8	60.7	132.7
Local Govs.	117	168	219	0.9	0.8	0.6	51	51	102	43.6	30.4	87.2
Priv. Gifts, etc.	1301	2077	3302	10.1	9.3	9.3	776	1225	2001	59.6	59.0	153.8
Endowment Income	590	1150	1877	4.6	5.1	5.3	560	727	1287	94.9	63.2	218.1
Educ. Activities	222	466	776	1.7	2.1	2.2	244	310	554	109.9	66.5	249.5
Indep. Operations	665	1198	2086	5.2	5.4	5.9	533	888	1421	80.2	74.1	213.7
Other Sources	3171	5688	9037	24.6	25.4	25.5	2517	3349	5866	79.4	58.9	185.0
Total Revenues	12868	22389	35416	100.0	100.0	100.0	9521	13027	22548	74.0	58.2	175.2

NOTES: "Other Sources" includes revenues generated by hospitals and auxiliary enterprises, as well as interest income and gains from investments or unrestricted current funds.

SOURCE: U.S. Department of Education, *Digest of Education Statistics*, various years.

Guaranteed Student Loan [GSL] volume during this time is not reflected in the federal revenue figures because these loans are privately financed and therefore are included in the tuition and fee revenue figures rather than in the federal funds category. This statistical treatment also helps to explain the growth between 1975 and 1985 in tuition and fees as a proportion of revenues.) State governments maintained their share of public sector funding between 1975 and 1985, whereas local government support fell off to some degree. At private institutions, a one percentage point decrease in annual private gifts as a proportion of revenues was offset by growth in the share of endowment income.

The following discussion examines trends in the major revenue sources other than tuition and fees: state funds in the public sector and endowment income and gifts at private institutions.

Funding and tuition trends in the public sector. One of the most interesting developments in the 1980s has been the relatively rapid increase in public sector tuition and fees, which, throughout most of the decade, increased just as fast as charges in the private sector, at an annual rate of about 10 percent. This pattern varies from the historical trend in which tuitions and fees in the public sector not only have tended to be much lower than those charged by private institutions, but also to have increased more slowly over time on a percentage basis. This historical difference in rates of change has contributed to the growing gap between public and private sector charges. In the 1980s, although the percentage growth in tuitions at public and private institutions have been similar, the fact that public tuitions are so much smaller than those in the private sector has meant that the gap between the two has continued to grow.

A number of officials at public colleges and universities have cited a slowdown in state funds as a primary reason why tuitions and fees at their institutions have increased so much in the 1980s -- much faster than has been the case historically. This argument about a shortfall in state funds and its impact on public sector tuitions has as its premise that public sector tuitions are typically set to fill any gap between state funding and institutional budgets. Thus, when state funding rises quickly relative to expenditures, the expectation is that tuitions will grow more slowly. When state funds are tight, on the other hand, it is reasonable to expect that tuition increases will have to be higher to meet the institutions' budgetary needs.

In nominal terms, state funding for higher education indeed has slipped in the 1980s relative to trends in the 1960s and 1970s, as Chart 7 indicates. Between 1965 and 1970, state appropriations grew by nearly 20 percent per year, and from 1970 to 1975, they grew by 13 percent per year. From 1975 to 1980,

CHART 7
PERCENTAGE CHANGE IN TOTAL AND PER-STUDENT
STATE FUNDING FOR HIGHER EDUCATION,
1965 TO 1985

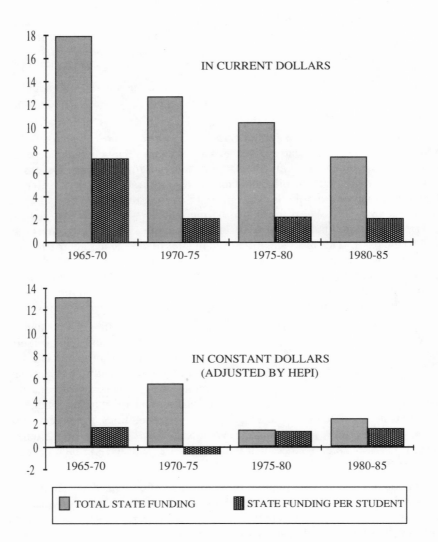

however, the increase in state funds dropped to 10 percent per year, and in the first half of the 1980s state funding grew at an average annual rate of only 8 percent. The same pattern is true when state funding is examined on a per-student basis. Here, the growth rate averaged 7 percent from 1965 and 1970 and only about 2 percent per year since 1970. This seems to confirm the perception that state funding of higher education has declined over time, and thus lends credence to the notion that a slowdown in the growth of state funding has led to the unusually rapid increase in public sector tuitions in the 1980s.

But when the state funding figures are adjusted for inflation, a different pattern emerges. Adjusted for the HEPI, state funding grew in real terms by 13 percent in the second half of the 1960s, dropped to 6 percent per year between 1970 and 1975, fell to about 1 percent per year between 1975 and 1980, but then increased nearly 3 percent per year between 1980 and 1985. The same pattern emerges for state funding per student, which actually declined in real terms in the early 1970s and has shown modest real increases since 1975. Thus, trends in state appropriations in constant dollars do not suggest a slumping in state support for higher education in the 1980s. This fact leaves us in somewhat of a quandary: If state higher education funding in real terms grew faster in the first half of the 1980s than in the last half of the 1970s, why have public sector charges increased faster in real terms in the 1980s?

To address the seeming inconsistency in the 1980s of simultaneous large tuition and funding increases in the public sector, it is necessary to consider year-to-year changes in public sector tuitions and funding rather than average changes over longer periods, such as five years. As Chart 8 clearly shows, state funding for higher education took a noticeable drop from 1980 through 1983; the growth in real terms was negative in each of those four years. A big spurt in funding in 1984 was followed by several years of modest growth, including 1986, when the funding increase was slightly negative in real terms.

The pattern of increase in public sector tuition and fees has not been uniform throughout the 1980s, as Chart 9 indicates. In 1981 and 1982, public college charges increased by double digits and registered substantial real increases. Since 1983, however, public sector charges have declined in both nominal and real terms. Although the average annual increase in public sector tuitions between 1980 and 1987 was close to 10 percent (5 percent in real terms), Chart 9 shows that this change was composed of very large increases in the first several years, followed by a steady decline.

When these annual percentage changes in tuitions are compared with changes over time in state funding per FTE student for higher education (as

CHART 8
ANNUAL PERCENTAGE CHANGES IN STATE
APPROPRIATIONS FOR HIGHER EDUCATION,
1966 TO 1987

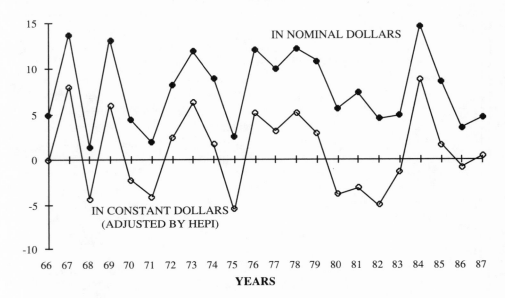

IN NOMINAL DOLLARS

IN CONSTANT DOLLARS
(ADJUSTED BY HEPI)

YEARS

CHART 9
ANNUAL PERCENTAGE CHANGES IN PUBLIC COLLEGE CHARGES
AND STATE APPROPRIATIONS PER FTE STUDENT, 1966 TO 1987

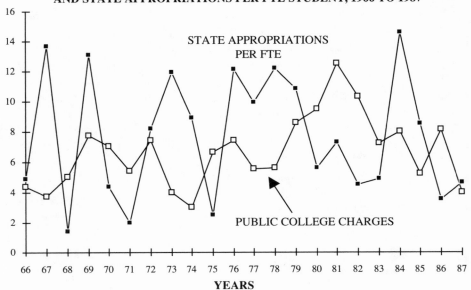

STATE APPROPRIATIONS
PER FTE

PUBLIC COLLEGE CHARGES

YEARS

shown in Chart 9), it is clear that the traditional inverse relationship between public sector charges and funding changes has continued in the 1980s. When funding has increased the most--for example, in 1972 through 1974, in the late 1970s, or in 1984--charges tended to increase more slowly. Conversely, when increases in state funding slowed in the early 1980s, the annual growth in tuitions and fees increased.

This logic suggests that public tuition patterns are likely to be an inverse function of general economic conditions. When the economy is doing well, state coffers fill up faster with revenues and therefore provide a greater base to pay for more higher education as well as for the other needs of the states. Conversely, if the economy takes a downturn, then state revenues will drop, funding for higher education will be restricted, and tuitions will need to increase faster to compensate for the slowdown in funding. It is hardly coincidental that the largest increases in public sector charges occurred in the early 1980s, when the nation was in the throes of a severe economic recession. As economic conditions improved, the rate of increase in college charges moderated.

This inverse relationship between general economic health and tuition increases should be viewed as a weakness in the way that public higher education is financed in this country. It seems highly inappropriate for public tuitions to increase the fastest when economic conditions are bad--when students and their parents can least afford to pay more for college. Similarly, when times are good and parents *can* afford to pay more, the traditional funding approach leads public tuitions to increase more slowly.

The traditional inverse relationship between public tuition increases and the economy may be changing in a number of states, however. The State Higher Education Executive Officers (SHEEO) organization reports that at least a dozen states by the end of the 1980s moved toward a system in which tuitions are tied formally either to the level of expenditures or to the amount of state funding at public institutions. In these states, students and their families in effect are being asked to pay a set proportion of the costs of their education. In some other states, while no formal mechanisms link tuitions and funding, prices now are set informally in direct relation to how much state funding is made available. In these states, students and families in effect are also being asked to pay a portion of the increase in what it costs to educate a student in the public sector.[15]

As we have noted, the traditional method of using tuitions to plug the gap between costs and state funding remains the dominant method for setting tuitions in most of the states. But if and when more states adopt formula-driven approaches to price setting in the public sector, we should see a breakdown in the inverse relationship between tuition and funding increases. Such a change could improve the overall financing of public higher education, in that students and their families would be asked to pay more during economic good times and to pay lesser increases, at least, when the economy turns sour.

The downside of this argument is that during economic slowdowns, public institutions are hit twice--once, as state funds become restricted, and then again, as tuition revenues drop because they are tied to public funding patterns. States could address this legitimate institutional concern by establishing reserve funds during economic good times, when state funds are growing, and then drawing on these reserves when state funds are constrained. In many states, the building of reserve funds is legally restricted, and many institutional finance officers would be reluctant not to spend all the money they were appropriated in a given year. For these and other reasons, reserve funds would be opposed in a number of quarters. Nonetheless, establishing reserve funds would represent prudent budgeting practice and would enhance the economic health of many institutions

It is also the case that not all states move in concert with the national economy. For example, oil-rich states like Texas and Louisiana fared much better than the rest of the nation in the mid-1970s when the energy crises hit, and suffered in the 1980s when the price of oil fell. As a result, tuitions at public institutions in those states rose much faster than the national average in the 1980s. If a system of reserves had been in place in the 1970s, the impact of declining oil prices on public sector charges could have been much less severe.

Nor are changing economic conditions the only reason for establishing a system of reserves. Revenue misestimates is another. In recent years, a number of states, especially in the Northeast, have experienced shortfalls in projected revenues that have severely affected their abilities to fund state programs, including higher education. Changing federal priorities also can lead to augmented state responsibilities for health care, welfare, and other programs. In the early 1980s, the Reagan administration's efforts to shift responsibilities back to the states came at the same time that the recession was squeezing state revenues. In addition, movements like California's Proposition 13 can have an impact on higher education, as local tax revenues are scaled back placing greater burdens on the state to provide functions previously assumed by the localities. These and other potential shifts in state revenues and funding patterns demonstrate the need for a flexible system in which reserves are available in higher education to cushion the blow.

Tuitions for out-of state students and other charges. One obvious means for public institutions to increase their prices and revenues without requiring more from state residents and taxpayers is to raise the tuitions they charge to students from other states. Such a policy would seem especially appropriate at those public institutions that have applications far exceeding the number of available slots.

Although it is widely perceived that public institutions have been rapidly increasing the tuitions they charge out-of-state students, the available data do not support this perception. The Higher Education Coordinating Board of the state of Washington has been collecting national data on tuition and fees at public institutions for the past two decades. This data source indicates that tuitions at public institutions for in-state students increased by 34 percent between 1983-84 and 1987-88, whereas the charges to out-of-state students increased 36 percent. This small difference in growth rates suggests that states are not as a policy matter raising the out-of-state tuitions charged at public institutions to raise more revenues.[16]

States are highly variable, however, in their tuition-setting policies in this regard. For example, Texas raised its nonresident tuition and fees by 150 percent between 1983-84 and 1987-88, but increased in-state rates by 90 percent. Indiana, on the other hand, raised its in-state tuition rates slightly faster than those for out-of-state students during that time.

Mandatory fees and room and board charges are other forms of nontuition revenues that may be used to take up the slack when state funds are scarce. In a number of states, the legislatures set tuition levels, whereas campus officials determine fee schedules. In other states, campus administrators set tuitions. In some states, campuses retain the tuitions they collect; in other states tuitions are sent directly to the state treasuries and then sent back to the campus through state appropriations.

Differences in administrative arrangements among the states may be influencing trends in the growth of tuition and fees. State legislators, as a rule, are less willing to raise tuitions than are campus officials, for a simple reason: Legislators do not want to offend the voters--both parents and students--by raising tuitions at state institutions, whereas campus administrators see higher tuitions as a source of more funds for the institution. As a result, in states where legislatures set tuitions, those tuitions may rise more slowly than in states where campus officials have that power. Concomitantly, tuitions also may increase faster in states where campuses are permitted to retain all or a portion of their tuitions.

By the same token, in some states, fees may have increased faster in an effort to make up for revenues "lost" by keeping tuitions in check. In

Massachusetts, for example, the legislature has the final say on how much tuition is charged at state institutions. There, the legislature held tuitions level between 1984 and 1987. But during that same period, campus administrators increased fees rapidly, so that the overall increase in tuition and fees was generally consistent with national tuition and fee trends. Similarly, tuitions at the State University of New York (SUNY) campuses have not increased since 1983, but room and board charges increased substantially, so that overall charges at SUNY institutions grew roughly in line with national increases in overall college charges.

What we have said here about the influence of different administrative structures on price increases in the public sector is largely speculative, we must note, because our comments are based on isolated observations. Nonetheless, these speculations could reasonably serve as a basis for additional research, perhaps most appropriately conducted by the SHEEO organization. This research might focus more systematically on the extent to which tuitions and other charges have increased at different rates in the various states, as well as on the reasons for the divergence in the growth of different types of charges.

Trends in endowment income and private gifts. Because tuitions constitute over half of all private institution revenues, a discussion of the influence of other revenue sources on pricing decisions is much more limited than in the public sector. The one additional revenue source worth examining for private institutions is the income derived from endowments and private gifts.

Income from endowments and private gifts at private institutions as a share of total revenues stayed relatively constant between 1975 and 1985 (see Table 6). The share of income from private gifts fell from 10 percent in 1975-76 to 9 percent in 1985-86. But endowment income grew by roughly the same percentage. As a result, income from private gifts and endowments combined remained level at 15 percent of total revenues from 1975-76 to 1985-86, suggesting that this revenue source has neither pressured private institutions to raise their tuitions nor allowed them to moderate increases in their charges.

The tremendous variation in the endowment holdings and income of private institutions, however, greatly affects the ability of individual institutions to rely on this source of revenue. For the 100 institutions that hold about three-quarters of all endowments, the income from endowments is a significant source of revenue that provides flexibility in how these institutions set their prices. The majority of colleges and universities, however, have less than $1 million in income from endowments. These institutions are not able to draw on endowment income in a significant way to keep their charges below costs per student, and thus this revenue source has little or no impact on tuition levels.

Over the past decade there has been a substantial increase in endowments at many public institutions that have established and expanded foundations as conduits for private gifts. Yet despite the rapid growth in public sector foundations and endowments, the available data still suggest that income from endowments and private gifts remains a very small proportion of all public sector revenues. Nonetheless, many private institutional officials worry that the growth of giving to public sector institutions will make their own fund-raising efforts that much harder.

"STUDENT AID LEADS INSTITUTIONS TO RAISE THEIR CHARGES"

Changes over time in the availability of student aid frequently have been cited as a primary cause of the increase in tuition and other charges. This argument, linking student aid and prices, has two very different components. One is that the availability of federal student aid has allowed and even encouraged institutions to raise their tuitions faster than they could have without the aid. The other theory is that decreases in federal student aid have forced institutions to help deserving students through internal aid programs, which they have funded through increased tuition levels. This section examines each of these arguments in turn.

Federal student aid and higher tuitions. William Bennett and other Department of Education officials in the Reagan administration made headlines by singling out federal student aid as one of the primary reasons for the rapid increases in college tuitions in the 1980s. Their theory was that ready availability of federal student aid allows colleges and universities to raise their prices freely, without having to consider the political or economic repercussions of requiring additional payments from students and their families. In this environment, students are said to be insulated from the effects of increased prices because of the increased aid they receive. Other critics have picked up on this theme by suggesting that federal aid funds tuition inflation just as the extent of federal reimbursement has led to the cost explosion in health care.

Although the assertion that the availability of student aid could be fueling tuition increases seems plausible on first inspection, the reality of how federal student aid works suggests that the theory is wrong for at least three reasons.

One is that only about half of the students enrolled in postsecondary education receive federal financial aid. In addition, many of those who receive aid get relatively little in the way of grant assistance. Therefore, federal aid insulates far less than half of all students from the impact of increased college charges. Thus, a majority of students do not receive any federal aid or receive relatively small amounts of aid; they are very directly affected when institutions raise their prices. These students are most likely to vote with their feet if charges at a particular institution become excessive. In any case, federal student aid does not insulate most students from feeling the effects of tuition increases, contrary to what many critics of the current system assert.

Second, the pattern of funding for student aid in recent years contradicts the scenario in which aid supposedly funds tuition growth. Student aid increased fastest in the 1970s, when increases in college charges were lagging behind inflation. In the 1980s, when college tuition and fees have been increasing at twice the rate of inflation, the growth in federal aid has slowed or turned downward in real terms. Thus, if anything, the historical pattern suggests that cuts in federal student aid lead to tuition increases. The rapid growth in the 1980s of aid provided by institutions lends a supporting rationale for why federal student aid may be inversely related to the growth in college charges.

In response to arguments about the inverse relationship between the growth of federal student aid and college charges, some have argued that federal student aid, as measured in certain ways, has continued to increase in real terms in the 1980s. As Table 7 indicates, federal student aid has increased in real terms when federally guaranteed loan volume is included in the measure, or when programs not administered by the Department of Education, such as Veterans Administration and Social Security educational benefits, are excluded. But the fact that federal student aid has increased in real terms in the 1980s does not disprove that an inverse relationship may have existed between federal student aid and increases in college charges. The relevant statistic from Table 7 is that all the measures of federal student aid increased less in real terms in the 1980s than in the 1970s, whereas real increases in college charges have been much larger in the 1980s than during the previous decade.

Finally, the best way to demonstrate that federal student aid does not generally lead to higher college charges is to examine how the federal programs work and the extent to which award levels are influenced by increases in tuition and other charges. That is, if an institution increases its charges, to what extent do its students then receive additional federal aid? In Pell Grants? In loans? In campus-based aid?

TABLE 7

CHANGES IN DIFFERENT MEASURES
OF STUDENT AID, 1970 TO 1987

CURRENT DOLLARS

Cumulative Changes (%)

	1970-75	1975-80	1970-80	1980-87	Total 1970-87
Total Student Aid	133	64	283	42	446
All Federal Aid	160	68	336	28	460
All Dept. of Ed. Aid	97	227	542	64	951
All Federal Student Loans	37	293	437	78	853
Specially Directed Federal Aid	221	-26	138	-64	-14
Student Aid Appropriations	342	90	741	77	1391

Average Annual Changes (%)

	1970-75	1975-80	1970-80	1980-87	Total 1970-87
Total Student Aid	18.5	10.5	14.4	5.2	10.5
All Federal Aid	21.0	10.9	15.9	3.6	10.7
All Dept. of Ed. Aid	14.5	26.7	20.4	7.3	14.8
All Federal Student Loans	6.4	31.5	18.3	8.6	14.2
Specially Directed Federal Aid	26.2	-5.8	9.0	-13.5	-0.9
Student Aid Appropriations	34.6	13.7	23.7	8.5	17.2

CONSTANT 1986 DOLLARS

Cumulative Changes (%)

	1970-75	1975-80	1970-80	1980-87	Total 1970-87
Total Student Aid	68	7	81	3	87
All Federal Aid	87	10	106	-7	91
All Dept. of Ed. Aid	42	113	203	19	259
All Federal Student Loans	-1	157	153	29	226
Specially Directed Federal Aid	131	-52	12	-74	-71
Student Aid Appropriations	219	24	296	29	409

Average Annual Changes (%)

	1970-75	1975-80	1970-80	1980-87	Total 1970-87
Total Student Aid	11.0	1.4	6.1	0.5	3.7
All Federal Aid	13.4	1.9	7.5	-1.0	3.9
All Dept. of Ed. Aid	7.2	16.4	11.7	2.5	7.8
All Federal Student Loans	-0.3	20.7	9.7	3.7	7.2
Specially Directed Federal Aid	18.3	-13.5	1.1	-17.4	-7.0
Student Aid Appropriations	26.1	4.4	14.8	3.7	10.1

SOURCE: The College Board, *Trends in Student Aid: 1963 to 1983 and 1980 to 1988.*

The answer to these questions is: not very much. The Pell Grant award for most recipients is determined by subtracting family resources from the maximum award. For these recipients, the cost of attending college plays absolutely no role in determining the size of their award. For the roughly one million Pell Grant recipients who have relatively little in the way of family resources and who attend lower-cost institutions, the award is based on 60 percent of their costs of attendance, as determined through program rules and regulations. For these students, changes in what colleges charge can make asmall difference in the amount of their award, although the amount of the increase in awards typically is no more than $100 to $200.

At one point, in response to comments that college charges made little difference in the size of Pell Grant awards, the Department of Education ran a computer simulation to estimate the impact on program costs of changes in college charges. The department's own estimate was that a 10 percent change in college charges resulted in a 1 percent change in Pell Grant awards. Some officials in the department concluded from this simulation that Pell Grants are "indexed" to college costs. A more realistic assessment, however, would be that a ratio of 1 to 10 for Pell Grants qualifies more as "no causation" than as "indexation."

In the Stafford (GSL) program, the potential for a relationship between college charges and student aid is greater because the size of the loan is need-based: it may not exceed a student's costs of attendance minus other resources. Under such a formula, increases in an institution's costs of attendance would lead to greater eligibility for aid; thus, the program formula is more supportive of the theory that aid and college charges are directly linked. Yet, typically, at least half of all Stafford borrowers receive the maximum amount allowed. For these students, a change in college costs makes no difference in the amount of loan received. As with the Pell Grant program, the Department of Education simulated the Stafford program to assess how much changes in college costs might affect levels of borrowing. The department's estimate was that a 10 percent change in price might result in a 5 percent change in borrowing. Although the relation of Stafford Loans to price changes therefore is greater than that of Pell Grants, it still is not high enough to justify the charge that student aid is "indexed" to college costs.

In the other major form of federal student aid--the campus-based programs of work-study, grants, and loans--virtually no connection can be drawn between the amount of aid provided and the change in costs. Although costs of attendance are included in the formula for determining how much aid an institution receives, this makes little or no difference in the amount of aid a student at that institution receives. The allocation of funds in the campus-based programs instead is primarily a function of how much the institution received the year before. Increased costs of attendance might mean that an institution (and its students) receives more funds, but this would generally happen only at the expense of less funds being provided to another institution. The more likely instance would be that an institution that increased its charges would find that it had a greater level of unmet need, because the need of its students had increased with the higher costs of attendance. But if the amount of total federal funds stayed roughly the same, the institution would continue to receive the same amount as before despite the increased "need" of its students.

For all federal student aid programs collectively, the above analysis would suggest that a 10 percent change in college charges results in about a 2 percent change in aid availability. This kind of tenuous relationship between college costs and federal student aid availability certainly would seem insufficient to support the contention that federal student aid has been a major factor in the surge of college charges.

Having confuted the argument that federal student aid and college costs are linked as a general matter, we should note that in a limited number of cases such a relationship probably does exist. Two particular examples come to mind. The first is for institutions that charge little or no tuition. In such cases, the institution is failing to maximize the use of federal student aid for its students. One example of this was the City University of New York, which through the early 1970s charged no tuition. When the New York fiscal crises of that time forced CUNY to charge tuition as a new source of revenue, the decision on how much to charge was affected to some degree by the realization that the net effect of the increase for many students would be small or nil because federal (and state) student aid would increase at the same time. This strategy of capturing federal student aid benefits through tuition increases is limited, however; after a certain point, increases in tuition no longer result in increased federal aid.

The other principal example of a linkage between college charges and federal student aid is in the proprietary sector, where many institutions apparently charge prices that reflect the availability of aid to their students. Available statistics suggest that many of these schools are setting their prices in close relation to the maximum awards in Pell Grants and Guaranteed Student Loans. For example, the average tuition for proprietary schools applying for federal campus-based aid was $1,700 in 1979-80 and $2,300 in 1987-88. The maximum Pell Grant was $1,800 in 1979-80 and $2,200 in 1987-88, indicating that proprietary school tuitions tracked amazingly well with increases in the Pell Grant maximums. Another piece of evidence is that the median cost of attendance, as reported by these proprietary schools, was between $4,000 and $4,500 in 1987-88, when the combined maximum award in Pell Grants and GSLs was approximately $4,500. Among the proprietary institutions that applied for campus-based aid funds in that year, more than one-third of the schools reported charging costs of between $3,500 and $5,500. These statistics should be used with care because the schools that apply for federal campus-based aid represent a small and nonrepresentative sample of the proprietary school universe. But the data do suggest that in the proprietary sector, tuitions and other charges are more linked to the availability of federal student aid than is true in other sectors of postsecondary education. [17]

These trends in tuition and aid are consistent with the fact that proprietary school students are more likely to participate in the federal student aid programs than are students enrolled in colleges and universities. A survey of student aid recipients in 1986-87 indicated that more than four-fifths of proprietary school students receive some form of federal student aid, whereas the proportion of students in the collegiate sector receiving aid is one-half or less. This kind of heavy dependence on federal aid as a source of revenue in the proprietary sector would seem to be an invitation to set prices in relation to aid.[18]

It seems ironic that this apparent linkage between what proprietary schools charge and student aid suggests that this sector of postsecondary education has increased its prices more slowly than colleges and universities in the 1980s because of the decline in real terms of the value of the maximum Pell Grant awards and loan limits. But this "benefit" of linkage for students may have faded in the latter part of the 1980s, as the stunning and troubling growth in the use of Supplemental Loans for Students (SLS) by proprietary school students probably means that this expanded aid availability is fueling larger tuitions at these schools.

The role of internally funded student aid. With the slowdown in the growth of federal student aid programs in the 1980s and the shift from grants toward loans, additional pressures have been placed on institutions to increase the amount of student aid they provide from their own funds. To the extent that this form of aid is paid for through higher tuitions charged to nonaided students, it would be fair to say that *declines* in federal aid have been an important contributing factor in overall increases in tuitions. What have been the trends in the student aid funded by institutions? What impact have they had on the "net price" that students and their parents face?

A number of officials at colleges and universities, particularly in the private sector, have indicated that the aid they provide to their students has increased substantially in the 1980s. But there has been little systematic information available on the amount of aid provided by institutions. One possible source of information is the applications that institutions make for federal campus-based student aid programs, on which colleges are asked to report how much in all forms of financial aid they provide to their students. As Table 8 shows, institutions applying for federal student aid funds reported that they had more than doubled the amount of aid they provide from their own resources between 1979-80 and 1986-87, from $2.2 billion in 1979-80 to $5.2 billion in 1986-87. Thus, it appears that colleges and universities have been increasing the aid they provide faster than the rate of general inflation and faster than the increase in their charges to students.

Internally funded aid is particularly important at private institutions because of the higher tuitions they charge. More than half of all internally funded aid is provided by private institutions, although they enroll only one-fifth of all college students. From 1979-80 to 1986-87, the student aid provided by private institutions from their own funds nearly tripled, twice as fast as the growth in private college charges. Figures from the National Postsecondary Student Aid Survey (NPSAS) indicate that roughly two-fifths of the undergraduates at private colleges and universities in 1986-87 received aid from the institution they attended. The average award to full-time undergraduates at private institutions was nearly $2,800, or 80 percent more than the average $1,550 Pell Grant they received.[19]

One way of measuring the impact of the growth in internally funded student aid is to look at the change over time in what colleges charge their students minus the aid they provide from their own resources. This "net price" calculation should provide some insight into the relative growth of the burden that students and their families face in paying for college. Table 8 indicates the change between 1979-80 and 1986-87 in college charges (tuition, fees, room, and board); internally funded aid per student; and net price, defined as college charges minus institutional aid.

At least two interesting observations can be drawn from Table 8. First, the reports from private institutions that they are increasing the amount of student aid they provide from their own funds are confirmed. Second, and more surprising, the increase in this form of aid does not appear to have much impact on the growth of the "net price" that students face. Although internally funded aid in the private sector clearly is increasing faster than what colleges charge their students, it still constitutes only about one-fifth of tuition and fees and

TABLE 8

COLLEGE CHARGES, INSTITUTIONALLY FUNDED STUDENT
AID, AND CHARGES NET OF AID, 1979-80 AND 1986-87

PUBLIC

	1979-80	1986-87	Cum. % Change	Annual % Change	Dollar Change
Institutional Aid (in millions)	1375	2776	102%	10.6%	1401
FTE Enrollment (in thousands)	6393	7225	13%	1.8%	N/A
Aid / FTE Student	215	384	79%	8.6%	169
Tuition and Fees Per FTE Student	583	1100	89%	9.5%	517
College Charges Per FTE Student	2165	3820	76%	8.4%	1655
Tuition and Fees Net of Student Aid	368	716	95%	10.0%	348
College Charges Net of Student Aid	1950	3436	76%	8.4%	1486

PRIVATE

	1979-80	1986-87	Cum. % Change	Annual % Change	Dollar Change
Institutional Aid (in millions)	850	2440	187%	16.3%	1590
FTE Enrollment (in thousands)	2095	2350	12%	1.7%	N/A
Aid / FTE Student	406	1038	156%	14.4%	633
Tuition and Fees Per FTE Student	3130	6230	99%	10.3%	3100
College Charges Per FTE Student	4912	9470	93%	9.8%	4558
Tuition and Fees Net of Student Aid	2724	5192	91%	9.6%	2467
College Charges Net of Student Aid	4506	8432	87%	9.4%	3925

TABLE 8 (Continued)

COLLEGE CHARGES, INSTITUTIONALLY FUNDED STUDENT AID, AND CHARGES NET OF AID, 1979-80 AND 1986-87

			TOTAL		
	1979-80	1986-87	Cum. % Change	Annual % Change	Dollar Change
Institutional Aid (in millions)	2225	5216	134%	12.9%	2991
FTE Enrollment (in thousands)	8488	9575	13%	1.7%	N/A
Aid / FTE Student	262	545	108%	11.0%	283
Tuition and Fees Per FTE Student	1212	2405	98%	10.3%	1193
College Charges Per FTE Student	2843	5207	83%	9.0%	2364
Tuition and Fees Net of Student Aid	950	1860	96%	10.1%	910
College Charges Net of Student Aid	2581	4662	81%	8.8%	2081

SOURCES: U.S. Department of Education, *Digest of Education Statistics,* 1987 (Tuition and FTE Enrollment data); American Council on Education, special analysis of Department of Education FISCOP data (Institutional Aid).

about one-seventh of college charges, when room and board are added to tuition and fees.

Because internally funded aid remains a relatively small share of college charges, the rapid growth in this form of aid has not led to a large difference in the rate of change in the "sticker price" that colleges charge and the "net price" that students actually face. Tuition and fees per student grew at annual rate of 10.3 percent between 1979-80 and 1986-87, whereas tuition and fees net of all internally funded aid--that is, net price--increased 9.6 percent per year. From these statistics, we could speculate that private sector tuitions might have grown seven tenths of one percentage point less per year if institutions had not increased the amount of aid they provided out of their own funds. When looked at from this perspective, it could be surmised that student aid funded by institutions has contributed seven-tenths of one percentage point per year to the growth in college charges.

Another way to look at this issue is to ask the question: What proportion of tuition increases were used to provide more internally funded aid? In answer, Table 8 indicates that between 1979-80 and 1986-87, tuition and fees per student at private institutions increased by $3,100. During that same time, internally funded student aid increased by $633 per student. Thus, the increase in the student aid provided by institutions accounted for about one-fifth of the total increase in tuition and fees. Using this logic, the aid provided by private institutions accounted for one-fifth of the increase in tuitions and fees, or two percentage points out of the annual increase of 10 percent in tuition and fees. These two analyses suggest that it is reasonable to suppose that internally funded aid accounted for less than one to as much as two percentage points of the annual increase in private sector tuition and fees.

"COMPETITIVE PRESSURES HAVE LED TO TUITION INCREASES"

The setting of tuitions is the point in the budget process at which trends in expenditures, revenues, and student aid come together. Much of what has been written or said about the tuition issue makes it seem that the tuition-setting decision is a natural and unchangeable consequence of expenditure and revenue trends at a given institution. For example, college administrators often cite faculty salary increases or the high costs of periodicals and laboratories as reasons why tuitions at their institution had to be increased. Or they say that shortfalls in other revenue sources such as state funding or alumni giving led to higher tuitions.

These kinds of explanations implicitly assume that budgetary pressures in the form of higher costs or lower revenues are the cause of higher college charges. But this one-way theory of institutional pricing runs counter to the common-sense notion that institutions have some control over their costs and their prices. It seems more reasonable to surmise that the relationship between tuitions and budgets is much more of a two-way street--one in which an institution's tuition income helps determine how much it can spend, and the institution's budget in turn feeds the tuition-setting decision.

It also is difficult to generalize about the tuition-setting process because colleges and universities use a wide variety of models to determine what they will charge their students. But the process in both the public and private sectors appears to be typically an interactive one between establishing a budget and setting a price. It typically involves the initial formulation of a budget, an estimation of available resources other than tuition, and an initial stab at tuition. Somewhere in the process the financial people do a reality check to see if their figures make sense by estimating what peer institutions are likely to charge their students and pay their faculty and other personnel. Before the final price is set and the letters go out, institutions are likely to make a number of adjustments in both the expenditure and revenue levels, as the overall budget figures are honed and the final tuition level is set.

Although the budget- and tuition-setting process is in many ways similar in the public and private sectors of American higher education, it is also dissimilar in several important ways. As we noted in the section on revenue sources, the primary determinant of tuition levels at public institutions appears to be the amount of funds the state provides. Because of the predominant role of state funding at public institutions, tuitions typically become the buffer that absorbs the difference between what the state provides and what institution would like to spend. This notion of public sector tuitions acting as a buffer suggests that they are set relatively late in the process, once the other pieces of the budget puzzle have been put in place. (This would be less true in states where tuition levels are tied by formula to funding or expenditure levels.) In addition, public campus administrators often do not have the responsibility for setting tuitions; that power frequently rests with the governor, legislature, or central governing board.

In contrast, the administrators or trustees at private institutions invariably are responsible for setting tuitions. In addition, private sector tuitions are a much larger share of total revenues. Therefore, private institution officials often may discuss tuitions earlier in the year than their public sector counterparts, because the amount of tuition collected will be a much larger determinant of their revenue base for the next year. This speculation may be worthy of additional research; that is, whether private sector tuitions generally are set earlier in the preceding year than in the public sector. In any case, the greater dependence on tuitions and the possible earlier time frame of tuition setting suggest that the following discussion of the tuition-setting process applies more to private colleges and universities than to public ones.

Choices in the tuition-setting process. The notion that tuition setting is a two-way street between expenditures and revenues depends in part on drawing a distinction between what an institution *must* spend and what it *chooses* to spend. Every college and university--public or private, small or large--must make certain expenditures to stay in operation. These mandatory expenditures include whatever long-term contractual obligations an institution may have. Compensating the faculty and other employees sufficiently to ensure that they do not go on strike or migrate to other forms of employment altogether might also reasonably be classified as a mandatory expenditure. Paying the utility bills so that the lights stay on and making the necessary expenditures and repairs to property are other components of mandatory spending. Also included are the expenditures required to comply with government regulations on health and safety, financial accountability, environmental pollution safeguards and cleanups, and affirmative action. The funds necessary to pay all these mandatory expenditures might be referred to as an institution's "base level" budget.

The level of tuition increase in a given year necessary to bring overall revenues in line with the base level budget may well be less than what the institution charged the year before; it might be the same; it might entail an increase to reflect inflation; or it might be higher than inflation. The base level budget and minimum tuition necessary to cover it will vary widely among institutions based on a great many factors. The degree of dependence on tuition and the size of endowment are two obvious considerations. The age of the institution and the size of its capital budget will be reflected in its expenditures for maintenance. The extent of long-term contractual obligations and the degree of unionization of faculty and other employees all will be reflected in the base level budget. The location and size of the institution could affect its utilities costs, its security budget, and many other items.

Beyond this base level budget and the amount of tuition necessary to cover it, whatever else an institution spends could be regarded as a matter of choice. If the faculty is to be given a real increase in salaries, if a new academic program is to be initiated, if a facility is to be built or renovated, or if more student aid is to be provided, the institution could be described as choosing to make expenditures that were not absolutely required for the continued operation of the institution. Certainly, in the short term, the college could continue to provide an adequate education and other services without making these additional expenditures.

The use of the term *choice* in this context, however, should not be equated with *unnecessary* or *frivolous*. For an institution to maintain or improve its faculty and its academic program, to upgrade its facilities, to expand its student services, or to provide more financial aid, it will require additional revenues. To the extent that tuitions are used to pay for these expenditures, the choices made in the tuition-setting process can be viewed as financing a portion of the increase above the base level budget.

Within this view of tuition setting as being at least partially a matter of choice, it is important to identify which factors influence administrators and trustees in deciding on the level of tuition increase at their institution. From the volumes that have been written or said about this subject, we know that many factors come into play. Basic issues include the following: How much would it cost to make improvements in the academic and nonacademic aspects of the institution? Where does the institution currently rank in terms of its faculty compensation relative to peer institutions, and where does it want to rank in the future? What are similar institutions going to charge next year, and where should an institution price itself relative to its competition? How sensitive are prospective students and their families to price increases, and will a tuition increase affect the composition of the next year's freshman class? In a related vein, how much financial aid is being provided, and how much more is needed to maintain a diverse student body?

The decisions made on these "choice" issues--what is spent on faculty, on student aid, on the construction and renovation of facilities, and the many other demands on resources--are critical in defining the "quality" of an institution. Colleges and universities can continue to do business and even to thrive while deciding not to raise their prices very much and by not extending themselves very far on the spectrum of additional expenditures. But over time, such self-constraint likely will detract from the quality of the education that is provided, especially if similar institutions are increasing their spending and investing more resources to meet their own needs.

It seems reasonable to assume that all college officials are interested in improving the quality of the education and related services they provide. But the capacity and willingness of students and their families to pay for these expenditures limits the extent to which administrators and trustees are able to raise tuitions to pay for these demands on institutional resources. It seems fair to assume that college administrators were just as interested in meeting these demands in the 1970s as they are today. The difference apparently is that in the 1980s, many college and university officials decided that they could increase their prices to meet these needs, and many did not feel this way in the 1970s.

The media have tagged this recent price-hiking behavior of American colleges and universities as "charging what the market will bear." A more accurate assessment of the trends of the past decade is that many institutions have decided to charge "*closer* to what the market will bear." This is especially true among the elite institutions, which, by all accounts, could charge substantially more than they do now and still attract students on the basis of benefits received from the education they provide in terms of intellectual enrichment and in employment opportunities after graduation. Second-echelon institutions that are charging nearly the same prices as the elites are more likely to be charging just about what the market will bear, and it seems reasonable to assume that stepped-up prices at these colleges would soon lead to reduced numbers of applications and enrollments. Some college officials now worry that the decline in applications that many private colleges experienced for the 1989-90 academic year is the first sign that the aggressive pricing policies of the 1980s may not work as well in the 1990s.

There is nothing inherently sinister or negative about the tuition-setting process as described above. With minor modifications, it describes the operation of any nonprofit organization that relies heavily on fees as a source of revenue. It is also very much in keeping with the good business practice of figuring out the demand curve for a product and then acting according to that assessment.

Nonetheless, the rapid run-up in tuitions over the past decade has been a significant source of "negativism" about American higher education. The process has been viewed as negative by the media and by consumers in part because of perceived excesses in what colleges are spending money on, or because of a focus on those aspects of the process that may seem exploitative or noncompetitive. For example, the perception that many institutions check what others are charging before they set their own prices--or worse, actively collude with others in the setting of tuitions--contributes to the negative image. To the extent that institutions have based their pricing decisions on the existence of a relatively inelastic demand curve, they have been accused of being greedy and of gouging their students and their families. Many colleges also have been criticized for their possibly excessive devotion in recent years to a marketing mentality, which runs counter to the perhaps antiquated notion that colleges should not be in the business of finding consumers or maximizing revenues.

The role of competition in the tuition-setting process. Each of these negative characterizations has a certain amount of validity, at least in describing the behavior of some institutions. But it also could be argued that higher education is being held to an excessive standard in this regard. If a college builds a new recreational facility because students have indicated a preference for it and parents appear willing to pay for it, should the college be chastised for doing so? Should an institution be criticized when it raises its tuition after it conducts a study that indicates that higher tuitions will not lead to significant shifts in its applicant pool or enrollees? Would society be well served if college officials threw up their hands and went out of business as the traditional college-age group diminished rather than "dirtying" their hands by marketing their product? The irony is that if a business did all these things, it would simply be remaining competitive, but when a nonprofit organization indulges in such activities, it is demeaning itself.

This brings us to the issue of competition and its possible role in the tuition-setting process. Contrary to the notion that colleges and universities operate in a protected environment devoid of competition, all available evidence suggests that the higher education "industry" is extremely competitive. There are more than 3,000 colleges and universities in this country. With the decline in the size of the traditional college-age group, a strong buyers' market has evolved so that most students today need not worry that they will not be able to attend college because of a scarcity of seats.

A reasonable premise is that the decline in the traditional college-age group in the 1980s should have led to restraint in the growth of tuitions, as institutions sought to compete for students through lower prices. Clearly what one would expect if this premise were true has not occurred, as tuition levels increased substantially in real terms in the 1980s.

The conclusion that seems most accurate and justified is that institutions have chosen to compete in ways other than price in trying to attract students to their campus. The most noticeable form of competition is in the construction or renovation of campus facilities. The past decade has been a remarkable period of reconstruction on both public and private campuses. Many of the institutions that fretted over growing deferred maintenance in the 1970s are now in the midst of a building or renovation boom. It seems clear that administrators and trustees at these institutions have decided that better facilities are useful in competing for students, and it appears that many students and their families are willing to pay for these facilities in the form of higher tuitions and other charges.

In a much-discusséd article entitled "Why is College So Expensive?", Barry Werth answers that colleges are expensive for "one reason only, Mr. and Mrs. America: You want it that way." Werth's article discusses how far some institutions have gone in the direction of facilities enhancement, including constructing luxurious recreational facilities and acquiring commercial real estate to help provide students with shopping opportunities. Obviously, most colleges have not gone to such lengths. But, to a lesser degree, it appears that many institutions decided that better facilities, financed in part by higher tuitions, were important to a winning strategy in the 1980s. [20]

Facilities enhancement is far from the only example of the growing impact of competition on the cost and price structure of American higher education, however. Another factor is the heightened competition for faculty in many of the sciences, engineering, business, and other high-demand fields. The bidding wars that now regularly occur between campuses for faculty clearly are contributing to increases in the underlying cost structure of many institutions.

Still another manifestation of competition in American higher education is the extent to which institutions continue to attempt to offer a full range of academic programs as well as other services to their students. Despite intensified cost pressures in the 1980s, most institutions were not willing to pare back their course offerings to any significant degree for fear of being less attractive to a broad range of prospective students. This would appear to be a clear case in which competitive pressures have outweighed the potential cost savings that could be achieved if institutions were more intent on pursuing their comparative advantage by dropping or curtailing lower priority programs.[21]

In certain regards, lack of competition also can help to explain the rapid growth of college costs and charges. Many of the goods and services that colleges and universities purchase are not commonly available. In some fields of study, there may be only a half-dozen experts in the whole country who meet the requirements of a particular institution. Much of the sophisticated equipment now being used in university laboratories is available only from a limited number of manufacturers. Similarly, for many of the periodicals that college and university libraries purchase the market is extremely limited, and the price is not set by normal supply and demand conditions. These instances of limited competition contribute to the potential for cost escalation.

Comparing the growth in expenditures and tuitions. One means for measuring or testing hypotheses about the relation between institutional budgets and the setting of tuitions is to compare the growth patterns of tuitions and expenditures over time. If budgets drive prices, we might reasonably expect to see a consistent pattern in which the growth of expenditures is consistently tied to the growth in tuitions. On the other hand, lack of an obvious correlation in the growth of tuitions and expenditures might suggest that factors other than cost-push economics play an important role in tuition-setting decisions.

The analysis of expenditures presented in this section differs from the traditional definition of spending in one important respect. We have defined expenditures here as the HEGIS category of education and general (E&G) expenditures minus what is reported on the HEGIS as spent for student aid. We also confine our analysis to expenditures per student to allow for consistency with the tuition and fee figures, which are stated on that basis. We have called this figure "education-related spending."

We excluded student aid from our analysis of expenditures for three reasons. First, the data reported on the HEGIS for student aid are notoriously bad. Definitions of what the HEGIS includes in the student aid account have not been consistent from year to year and often are not consistent with the actual use of the funds. Second, and much more important, student aid is not an expenditure in the same sense as salaries, fringe benefits, facilities and maintenance costs, and utilities, which involve an actual payment to an individual or an organization other than the educational institution itself.

Student aid provided by the institution is more appropriately categorized as a discount from the price and a subtraction from the revenues that the institution otherwise would have received. In that sense, student aid provided by the institution should appear as a deduction from revenue rather than as an additional expenditure. For example, suppose an institution decides to raise its tuition by $1,000 and then gives each student a $1,000 grant. Clearly, the situation of the students has not changed at all -- price net of aid has not been altered -- but conventional accounting would show an institution with $1,000 per student more in revenues and expenditures. Finally, in attempting to ascertain the amount of expenditures that relate to the cost of educating a student, it seems reasonable to exclude student aid, which does not have a direct impact on the content of the education that a student receives.

The fact that we have excluded student aid from the expenditure analysis in this section should not be interpreted to mean that student aid is unimportant in explaining the source of recent tuition increases. On the contrary, it is a critical part of the story, as our section on student aid suggests. Nor does our particular definition of education-related expenditures materially affect the conclusions we may draw about spending trends. As Table 9 indicates, between 1975 and 1985 there was very little difference in the growth of three different measures of expenditures: total (or current funds) expenditures, E&G expenditures, and education-related expenditures (E&G spending net of student aid). As the table also indicates, the use of aggregate or per-student expenditure figures makes very little difference in the comparison of the three different measures of expenditures because there was relatively little growth in enrollments during these years.

Table 10 and Chart 10 compare annual changes between 1976-77 and 1985-86 in tuition and fees and education-related expenditures per student at different types of institutions to determine the degree to which the growth in spending may explain changes in price over time. Between 1976 and 1985, tuition and fee charges rose about one-half of a percentage point per year faster than education-related expenditures per student in both the public and private sectors. But the pattern in the late 1970s differed from that of the early 1980s. Annual percentage increases in tuition and fees from 1980 to 1985 were substantially larger than increases in expenditures. At public institutions, tuitions increased more than two percentage points per year faster than expenditures. At private institutions, the increase in tuitions was one and a half percentage points per year greater than the increase in expenditures per student. This pattern, in which tuitions increased faster than expenditures in the 1980s, held true for each type of institution--universities, other four-year institutions, and two-year colleges--in both the public and private sectors.

In contrast, from 1976-77 to 1980-81 expenditures per student tended to increase faster than tuitions and fees, and the patterns at different types of institutions were more mixed than in the 1980s. At public institutions, expenditures in the late 1970s grew more than two percentage points per year faster than tuition and fees; at private institutions, expenditures grew slightly faster than tuition and fees between 1976 and 1980. While there was virtually no difference in the rate of increase in tuition and fees and expenditures at public universities, the largest difference in the growth of tuitions and expenditures was registered at other public four-year institutions, where education-related expenditures increased nearly twice as fast as tuitions. At private universities, expenditures increased one percentage point per year faster than tuition and fees, whereas there was very little difference in the increase in expenditures and tuitions at public four-year institutions, and at private two-year colleges tuition and fees grew much faster than expenditures.

TABLE 9

PERCENTAGE INCREASES IN DIFFERENT MEASURES OF EXPENDITURES, 1975-76 TO 1985-86

	% Change 1975-76 to 1980-81			% Change 1980-81 to 1985-86			% Change 1975-76 to 1985-86		
	Current Dollars	Constant '85/HEPI	Constant '85/CPI	Current Dollars	Constant '85/HEPI	Constant '85/CPI	Current Dollars	Constant '85/HEPI	Constant '85/CPI
AGGREGATE									
E&G Expenditures	63.6	14.1	6.9	52.0	4.3	16.5	148.8	19.0	24.5
Education Related Expenditures	64.2	14.5	7.3	51.3	3.8	15.9	148.5	18.9	24.3
Total Expenditures	64.6	14.8	7.5	52.3	4.5	16.6	150.7	19.9	25.4
PER FTE STUDENT									
E&G Expenditures/FTE	60.1	11.6	4.6	50.3	3.1	15.1	140.5	15.1	20.3
Education Related Expend./FTE	60.7	12.0	4.9	49.5	2.6	14.5	140.2	14.9	20.2
Total Expenditures/FTE	61.0	12.3	5.2	50.5	3.3	15.3	142.4	15.9	21.3

NOTE: "Total Expenditures" is elsewhere referred to as Current Funds Expenditures.

SOURCE: U.S. Department of Education, *Digest of Education Statistics*, 1988.

TABLE 10

CHANGES IN EDUCATION RELATED EXPENDITURES AND TUITION AND FEES PER FTE, BY TYPE AND CONTROL OF INSTITUTION, 1977-78 TO 1985-86

	1977-78	1978-79	1979-80	1980-81	1981-82	1982-83	1983-84	1984-85	1985-86	Average Annual Change		
										1977-78 1980-81	1980-81 1985-86	1977-78 1985-86
Public 2-Year												
Expenditures	8.1%	11.0%	8.0%	6.2%	9.5%	0.7%	6.4%	15.7%	8.0%	8.4%	8.0%	8.1%
Tuition and Fees	8.1%	6.9%	8.6%	8.5%	12.2%	9.5%	11.6%	10.6%	6.2%	8.0%	10.0%	9.2%
Public 4-Year												
Expenditures	8.2%	11.0%	11.1%	9.7%	9.3%	3.8%	6.0%	11.8%	8.2%	10.6%	7.8%	8.8%
Tuition and Fees	5.7%	4.4%	6.4%	8.9%	12.8%	15.1%	12.4%	6.2%	7.4%	6.6%	10.7%	9.1%
Public University												
Expenditures	8.0%	11.6%	8.8%	9.0%	7.9%	6.3%	7.2%	10.8%	8.8%	9.8%	8.2%	8.8%
Tuition and Fees	6.8%	5.6%	8.1%	8.9%	13.9%	11.7%	10.3%	7.9%	8.9%	7.5%	10.5%	9.4%
ALL PUBLICS												
Expenditures	8.0%	11.7%	9.5%	8.2%	8.7%	3.2%	6.6%	13.3%	8.6%	9.8%	8.0%	8.7%
Tuition and Fees	6.9%	6.1%	7.4%	8.6%	13.9%	10.7%	11.7%	9.0%	7.1%	7.3%	10.4%	9.3%

TABLE 10 (Continued)

CHANGES IN EDUCATION RELATED EXPENDITURES AND TUITION AND FEES PER FTE, BY TYPE AND CONTROL OF INSTITUTION, 1977-78 TO 1985-86

	1977-78	1978-79	1979-80	1980-81	1981-82	1982-83	1983-84	1984-85	1985-86	Average Annual Change		
										1977-1980	1980-1985	1977-1985
Private 2-Year												
Expenditures	0.6%	12.1%	7.6%	10.2%	6.8%	9.6%	3.4%	15.8%	5.6%	10.0%	8.2%	8.8%
Tuition and Fees	7.2%	7.3%	12.6%	17.0%	11.8%	11.5%	3.0%	12.5%	7.9%	12.3%	9.3%	10.4%
Private 4-Year												
Expenditures	6.5%	8.9%	11.5%	10.9%	10.8%	8.8%	7.7%	8.9%	8.1%	10.4%	8.9%	9.4%
Tuition and Fees	7.2%	10.0%	9.0%	12.3%	13.7%	12.3%	9.2%	8.7%	8.1%	10.4%	10.4%	10.4%
Private University												
Expenditures	5.2%	9.1%	11.7%	11.6%	9.2%	7.3%	11.8%	9.7%	8.8%	10.8%	9.4%	9.9%
Tuition and Fees	6.2%	7.6%	9.3%	12.2%	14.3%	14.2%	11.4%	10.1%	8.9%	9.7%	11.7%	11.0%
ALL PRIVATES												
Expenditures	5.8%	9.1%	11.6%	10.9%	9.8%	7.6%	9.6%	9.6%	8.5%	10.5%	9.0%	9.6%
Tuition and Fees	6.4%	9.3%	9.2%	11.8%	13.6%	11.8%	9.3%	9.5%	8.2%	10.1%	10.5%	10.3%

NOTES: "Expenditures" is defined in this table as Education and General Expenditures, less student aid. Data in this table may differ slightly from data appearing in other tables.

SOURCES: U.S. Department of Education, background tables used to prepare *Digest of Education Statistics*, 1988 (Expenditures); U.S. Department of Education, *Digest of Education Statistics*, 1987 (Tuition and Fees).

Chart 10 indicates the changing relationship between tuition and expenditure increases over time. In the late 1970s, expenditure increases consistently exceeded the growth in tuition and fees at public institutions; the pattern was more mixed at private institutions. In the early 1980s, tuition increases substantially exceeded the increase in expenditures at both public and private institutions. From 1981 to 1985, expenditure increases once again exceeded the growth in tuition at public institutions, whereas private sector expenditures and tuitions grew at the same rate

Of six institutions studied by Michael O'Keefe in the *Change* magazine article previously cited, four had a larger increase in tuition and fees than in expenditures per student between 1975-76 and 1985-86.[22] At the other two institutions, spending per student increased faster than tuition and fees, although in one case the real increase in tuitions and fees was only 1 percent over the 10 year period. It is worth noting, however, that the two institutions with the largest increase in expenditures per student were also the two with the largest increase in tuition and fees.

Notwithstanding this last example, the experience over the past decade seems to lend strong credence to the argument that expenditure patterns do not necessarily drive the degree of annual change in tuitions and other charges. Expenditures increased faster than tuitions and fees in the latter 1970s in virtually all types of institutions, whereas increases in expenditures per student lagged uniformly behind tuition increases in the first half of the 1980s. No pattern is discernible that would suggest an unvarying relation between the rate at which expenditures increase and how much institutions increase what they charge their students.

The data clearly indicate that at least in the first half of the 1980s tuitions increased faster than expenditures. The natural question to ask is: What are these increased revenues being used for? To answer this question, we need to return to our discussion at the beginning of this study concerning the difference between costs and price. Because the price of a higher education is typically much smaller than expenditures per student, the two can increase at much different percentage rates.

Consider, for example, a college that in a given year charges $5,000 per student and spends $10,000 per student. Further assume that the institution has a policy of not offering any financial aid to its students. If in the next year that institution decides to increase its tuition by $1,000, tuition will have increased by 20 percent ($1,000 divided by $5,000). If the institution then fully uses this $1,000 in new tuition to pay for increased faculty salaries or to create a new

CHART 10
ANNUAL PERCENTAGE CHANGE IN
EDUCATION-RELATED EXPENDITURES
AND TUITION AND FEES PER STUDENT,
1976-77 TO 1985-86

PUBLIC INSTITUTIONS

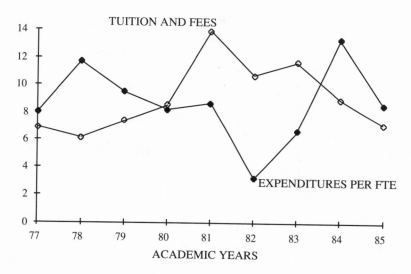

PRIVATE INSTITUTIONS

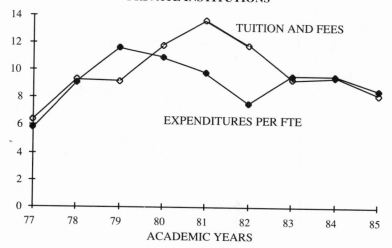

department in biochemistry, spending per student will have increased by 10 percent ($1,000 increase over the initial $10,000 cost per student). Thus, the same dollar increase in tuition and spending results in much different percentage changes in the two items.

Suppose, to vary our example, that the college decides to use half of its $1,000 increase in tuition to pay faculty salary increases and the other half to establish its own program of student aid. In this instance, the college's tuition, as it appears in the catalog, again will have risen by 20 percent ($1,000 increase over the initial $5,000 price). But education-related expenditures will have increased by only 5 percent (a $500 increase over the $10,000 cost per student). And the price charged to students net of financial aid will have increased by 10 percent ($6,000 in new tuition minus $500 in new aid divided by the original $5,000 sticker price).

These scenarios confirm that it is perfectly plausible, even to be expected, that college charges will increase over time at a rate different from the increase in expenditures per student. They also suggest that perhaps more attention should be paid to the changes over time in the net price of college--the sticker price of tuition and other charges minus the aid provided--as a measure of the change in prices that students and their families actually face.

In this process, the level at which tuition is set, therefore, depends on a number of factors in addition to how much it costs to educate a student at a particular institution. In the public sector, the principal consideration is how much funding the state provides. For private institutions, noncost factors that affect pricing decisions include how much endowment and other income are available to pay for costs, what peer institutions charge their students, and an estimation of what the "traffic" will bear.

Because of the variations in how tuitions are set, it is difficult if not impossible to identify a single reason why prices increased at a rate faster than expenditures per student in the 1980s. At some institutions, it appears to be a matter of "follow the leader." When one price-leading college raises its tuition by a certain percentage, peer institutions may follow. The reason the price leader raised its tuitions may have little or nothing to do with the situation of the price followers. The result is that the price increases at some institutions will be consistent with their cost structure, whereas at others they will not.

Another aspect of the tuition-setting process has to do with the value of a college education, as perceived by students, in general and at particular institutions. Data collected by the Bureau of the Census as part of its Current Population Survey suggest that the rate of return for a college education, as measured by the difference in earning power between college and high school graduates, increased in the 1980s. To a large extent, this growing disparity in incomes appears to be mostly a function of the fact that the incomes of high school graduates have declined more rapidly in real terms than have those of college graduates.[23]

This growing difference in the economic returns to education is a condition that indirectly may have contributed to the recent rapid increase in tuitions. To the extent that students and their families perceive a greater economic benefit from going to college, they may be willing to pay a higher price for the education they receive. Under this theory, although college tuitions are unarguably high, they may still be a bargain relative to the economic value to the student of the education received.

This argument relates to the fact that with the rapid increase in college charges in the 1980s, the tuition-setting process was the focus of increased political attention. Former secretary of education William Bennett and other critics described college officials as greedy and irresponsible for raising their tuitions at such a sharp rate in the 1980s. Although their concern about the large increase in college charges is surely justified, it seems hollow coming from individuals ostensibly committed to free market principles who have been so quick to comment on the economic value that accrues to students who go to college.

In this context, speculate about what would happen if a social and economic conservative were appointed as the president of either a public or private university. Would not such a conservative attempt to increase substantially the tuitions charged at that institution? At a public university, the conservative president surely would argue that state subsidies are much too large and should be greatly reduced, with a consequent large increase in the tuitions charged to students. Moreover, as president at either a public or private institution, such a conservative presumably would argue that the economic value to the student in the form of increased earnings over a lifetime are enormous and should be reflected in the price that students pay for the education they receive. Of course, the conservative president would contend that the growth in tuitions could be restrained by keeping costs down. But even with cost efficiencies, the reign of a conservative as college president undoubtedly would include steeper tuitions.

This brief discussion of the components of the tuition-setting process has not been intended as a comprehensive analysis of how colleges and universities set their prices. That subject can, and has, filled entire volumes. Our purpose here has been to point out that college tuitions are not strictly a function of institutional costs and administrative greed, and that simplistic explanations of the tuition-setting process are not terribly helpful in advancing the level of the debate over college costs.

THE DECLINE IN THE TRADITIONAL COLLEGE-AGE GROUP: A CROSSCUTTING FACTOR?

At the beginning of the 1980s, the traditional college age group of 18- to 24-year-olds peaked at approximately 30 million. Since then, this age group has declined by about 15 percent, and it will decrease by another 10 percent before the trend bottoms out in the mid-1990s. The 1980s also were a time when college tuitions began to increase at unprecedented rates. Are these two trends merely coincidental, or does the decline in the size of the traditional college-age group help explain why college prices shot up in the 1980s?

In the 1970s there were predictions that the decline in the number of 18- to 24-year-olds could spell disaster for American higher education in the 1980s. The postwar expansion in enrollments, in which the number of college students more than quintupled--from 2 million in 1950 to 12 million in 1980--was expected to stop, and the possibility existed that college enrollments would decrease. There also were predictions of widespread closings of colleges and universities that, unmindful of the inevitable reversal in the number of college-age youth at the end of the baby boom, had overbuilt in the 1960s and 1970s. These predictions often were discussed in the context of how higher education would deal with a decade or more of steady-state conditions, after several decades of remarkable growth.

The predicted decline in the size of the American higher education establishment, we now know, has not materialized. Rather than falling, enrollments have stabilized over the past decade and actually have moderately increased about 1 percent per year. A handful of institutions have closed, and several dozen have merged with others, but the number of higher education institutions actually has increased slightly over time.

Several factors contributed to the unexpected stability in enrollments in the 1980s. The proportion of the college age group that attend college for at least one year increased somewhat; now more than one-half of all high school graduates can be expected to go on to some form of postsecondary education. In addition, the trend over the past several decades, in which an increasing proportion of older students enroll in college, has continued. Today nearly 40 percent of students enrolled in college are 25 years of age or older, up from just over 30 percent in 1980, and this trend is predicted to continue so that by the end of the century it may be the case that over half of all college students are 25 or older.

That higher education has avoided the disaster of falling enrollments has been recounted frequently. But less discussed have been the ways in which the shrinkage in the size of the traditional college-age group may have contributed to the explosion in college costs and prices that we witnessed in the 1980s. There are at least three reasons why the presence of fewer 18- to 24-year-olds in the college population may translate into higher costs and prices: the inability of colleges to capture increasing economies of scale, the increased costs of recruitment, and the economic impact of fewer college graduates of traditional age entering the labor market. These three reasons touch in one way or another on each of the five explanations for increasing college costs discussed in this study. In that respect, it is possible that the decline in the size of the traditional college-age group may be a crosscutting or unifying explanation for why college charges increased in the 1980s.

The leveling in enrollments. After several decades of rapid growth, enrollments in higher education have remained relatively level since the mid-1970s. As we noted in the section on why higher education expenditures have increased, the leveling in enrollments seems to have prevented institutions from capturing the economies of scale associated with growing enrollments and, as a result, may have contributed to the rapid growth in per-student spending that occurred in the 1980s. It is easy to imagine that the 8 percent annual expenditure increase of the 1980s could have been more in the neighborhood of 5 to 6 percent if the patterns of increasing enrollments in the early 1970s had continued. Under such a circumstance, the resulting increase in price might reasonably have been 7 to 8 percent, rather than the 10 percent figure registered in the 1980s.

A principal reason why higher education enrollments have plateaued over the past decade is the leveling of the numbers of traditional college-age group in the late 1970s and their decline in the 1980s. Without the growth in the number of students graduating from high school, enrollments in colleges and universities have come to a standstill. The small increase in the college enrollment rates of these students has not nearly compensated for the decline in the size of the group in the 1980s. In fact, the decrease in the number of traditional college-age youth would have led to a decline in higher education enrollments if the participation of older nontraditional students had not increased markedly. Thus, we can infer that the decline in the traditional college-age group, through its impact on enrollment trends, had a rather direct effect on the pattern of college spending and charges in the 1980s.

The increased costs of recruitment and retention. Another result of a smaller college age group may be in the higher costs of recruitment and retention. Colleges and universities in the 1960s and early 1970s enjoyed a sellers' market. It was typical for students to apply to a number of institutions in the hope that at least one would accept them. The competition for admission into a wide range of schools was fierce. But with the leveling in the size of the traditional college-age group in the late 1970s and its decline in the 1980s, the market advantage increasingly shifted from the colleges to the students.

This shift has had at least two obvious consequences in college and university cost and price structure that have been mentioned in previous sections of this study. One is that institutions today invest much more in marketing than they ever did before. Today's colleges commonly send packets of printed materials to applicants, have enlarged their admissions staffs, and have taken other steps designed to lure students to their campuses. No doubt, these steps have accelerated the steep rise in the administrative costs of many institutions over the past decade.

Increased use of institutionally funded student aid could be interpreted as another indicator of higher recruitment costs. The need analysis system that is used to award most student financial aid was developed in the 1950s, when the growing competition for students led to unseemly and counter productive bidding for students through aid that was unrelated to the need of the student. In the 1960s and 1970s, institutions adhered more closely to need-based principles because most colleges and universities had more than enough applicants to fill their seats. The renewed increase in competition for students in the 1980s brought some fraying in the adherence to need-based principles and a resurgence in the amount of non-need-based aid, although not nearly to the same degree as in the 1950s.

Changing demographics may have had an effect on the costs of retention as well as recruitment. The growing numbers of nontraditional students who have entered higher education in recent decades typically require larger amounts of support services to complete their education than do an equivalent number of traditional full-time students. In addition, nontraditional students often don't purchase some of the services that generate income for institutions, such as housing and food services. Thus, it is reasonable to argue that the net costs to institutions of retaining students through graduation have increased as the numbers of traditional college-age students have declined.

The changing economic prospects for college graduates. In the 1970s, it was popular to discuss the declining economic value of a college degree, and a number of books and articles on the subject reinforced the point. These public discussions no doubt led some students and their families to reconsider the wisdom of pursuing a college education. It seems reasonable to assume that this climate of skepticism also had an impact on college administrators as they made their tuition decisions. Large scale increases in tuition are not likely to succeed when there is widespread doubt regarding the value of a college education. Thus, it may have been more than a coincidence that tuitions increased less than inflation in the 1970s, when the perceived value of a college education was declining.

Recent studies indicate that in the 1980s, the economic return to a college education has substantially rebounded with college graduates now commanding far better salaries than high school graduates. One reason for this rebound may be the decline in the traditional college-age population. As the number of traditional college-age students has declined over the past decade, the growth in the number of college graduates has slowed. Meanwhile, the number of jobs that require a college education has grown at a rapid rate. Employers appear to be bidding up salaries and benefits in an effort to recruit the best-educated workers to fill these jobs. As a result, college graduates are now in a much better negotiating position than they were in the 1970s, when the number of graduates seemed to exceed the number of well-paying jobs.

As word gets out that the economic prospects of college graduates are improving, demand for a college education also increases. In this favorable environment, colleges are likely to increase their tuitions faster than when interest in college is flagging. This logic, drawn from basic economic theory, suggests that there is at least an indirect link between the tuitions that colleges charge and the incomes that their graduates receive.

Many college administrators would deny that such a connection exists. They would assert that their pricing decisions are made without reference to the income of college graduates. Nonetheless, human nature being what it is, it seems unrealistic to expect that those who set tuitions could be completely unmindful of the changing demand for the product they are offering, and indirectly of the changing economic prospects of the students they are educating.

Endnotes

[1] By far, the largest single item in the HEPI is the salaries, wages, and benefits paid to professors and other professional staff as well as support staff and other nonprofessionals. Faculty salaries alone account for over two-fifths of the index. Other professional salaries exceed one-tenth, and nonprofessional wages and salaries represent one-sixth of the index weighting. Fringe benefits compose nearly one-tenth of the total HEPI. The total weight in HEPI for all personnel compensation including nonprofessional wages and salaries and fringe benefits is roughly four-fifths. Other items in the remaining one-fifth of the HEPI weights include contracted services, equipment, supplies, books and periodicals, and utilities.

[2] *Higher Education Prices and Price Indexes: 1987 Update* (Washington, D.C.: Research Associates of Washington, 1987).

[3] Another criticism of the HEPI is that the weights used to estimate it are based on institutional expenditure patterns as they existed in the early 1970s when the index was first developed. To the extent that those spending patterns have changed, the HEPI may not accurately reflect the prices that colleges and universities face today. Typically, however, the weights used for indexes are not revised frequently because it is then more difficult to isolate the effects of changing expenditure patterns from changes caused by the increasing cost of the various index factors. The market basket used for the CPI, for example, traditionally has been changed only once every couple of decades, although the time between CPI reweightings is being shortened. In that respect, experience with the CPI would suggest that a reweighting of the HEPI probably is warranted. Although the spending patterns in higher education have changed to some degree since the early 1970s, however, they probably have not changed enough so that a reweighting of the HEPI would result in a large change in the index trends.

[4] There are two principal sources for statistics on faculty salaries, and both support this characterization of the relationship between salaries, tuitions, and prices since the early 1970s. One is the American Association of University Professors (AAUP), which has collected time series data on faculty salaries since 1971-72. The National Center for Education Statistics of the U.S. Department of Education also collects data on faculty salaries, as reported in *Salaries, Tenure, and Fringe Benefits of Full-Time Instructional Faculty.*

[5] Data collected by College and University Personnel Association, as reported in the *Chronicle of Higher Education,* July 6, 1988

[6] Information on part-time faculty is from U.S. Department of Education statistics cited in Phyllis Franklin et al., "When Solutions Become Problems: Taking a Stand on Part-Time Employment," *Academe* (May-June 1988).

[7] Data on the age of faculty members traditionally has been very limited. But William G. Bowen and Julie Ann Sosa, in *Prospects for Faculty in the Arts and Sciences,* (Princeton University Press, 1989) have constructed a faculty age distribution from the Survey of Doctorate Recipients data collected by the National Research Council. The analysis in Chapter 2 of their report indicates that 40 percent of faculty members were 50 years or older in 1987, compared to less than 30 percent in 1977.

[8] *op cit.* p.71

[9] Chester E. Finn, Jr., "Judgment Time for Higher Education," *Change* (July/August 1988), p.37.

[10] Williams was one of the six institutions studied in Michael O'Keefe, "Where Does the Money Really Go?" *Change* (November/December 1987), pp. 12-34.

[11] John Dunn and Dawn Geronimo Terkla, "When is it Going to Stop?: A Speculation on Tuition Rates at One Private University," paper prepared for the 15th Annual Conference of The North East Association for Institutional Research, Providence, R.I. October 23-35, 1988.

[12] U.S. Department of Education, *Higher Education Administrative Costs: Continuing the Study* (Washington, D.C.: January 1988).

[13] For a description of the view from campus of the effects of government regulation and litigation, see Marvin Greenberg, "What's Happened to College Tuitions and Why: A View from the Public University," *The College Board Review* (Spring 1988), pp.13+. For an analysis of the costs of regulation in an earlier time, Carol Van Alstyne (Frances) and Sharon Coldren prepared a study for ACE in the mid-1970s, "The Costs of Implementing Federally Mandated Social Programs at Colleges and Universities," American Council on Education, (Washington, D.C.: June 1976).

[14] *Digest of Education Statistics 1988,* Table 247, p. 281

[15] Changes in the way that states set tuitions in relation to costs are discussed in State Higher Education Executive Officers, "Report on Survey of State Practices," unpublished paper, 1988.

[16] Higher Education Coordinating Board, State of Washington, "1987-88 Tuition and Fee Rates - A National Comparison," February 1988.

[17] Data on proprietary schools are extremely limited. These figures on proprietary school tuition and total costs of attendance are drawn from tabulations of reports submitted to the Department of Education by proprietary schools applying for federal campus-based student aid funds.

[18] U.S. Department of Education, National Postsecondary Student Aid Survey

[19] ibid.

[20] Barry Werth, "Why is College So Expensive?" *New England Monthly* (January 1988), pp. 35-43.

[21] Arnold Weber eloquently makes this and other points in "Colleges Must Begin Weighing Public Perceptions, as Well as Economic Reality, When Setting Tuition," *The Chronicle of Higher Education,* October 11,1989, page A52

[22] O'Keefe, *op cit.*

[23] Chart 2:8 in *The Condition of Education: Postsecondary Education, 1988,* U.S. Department of Education, demonstrates this point about the growing disparity between the incomes of college and high school graduates. For a good recent analysis of this trend, see Kevin Murphy and Finis Welsh, "Wage Premiums for College Graduates: Recent Growth and Possible Explanations," *Educational Researcher,* Volume 18, Number 4, May 1989, pp. 17-26.

Chapter 3

FUTURE PROSPECTS FOR COLLEGE TUITION INCREASES

The past decade's rapid increase in college charges relative to inflation raises an obvious question: Will tuition increases in the future continue to outpace inflation by a large margin, or can we expect to see a return to the historical pattern in which college charges tended to exceed inflation by only a percentage point or two per year?

If trends in the size of the traditional college-age group are a major determinant of what it costs to educate a college student and what colleges charge for tuition, then perhaps we should not expect a return to the more traditional relationship between college prices and inflation, at least not until the college-age group begins to increase again in the mid-1990s.

Until then, we may expect to see a continuation of the pattern in which colleges are unable to spread increased costs over larger numbers of students; incur higher costs per student; and, as a result, raise their prices. In addition, costs for recruitment are likely to remain high as long as the applicant pool continues to dwindle through the middle of the 1990s. It also seems probable that internally funded aid paid for through increased tuitions will grow, as institutions continue their efforts to attract students by offering increased aid. The recent trend of increasing rates of return for education probably will not abate in the foreseeable future, as the demand by employers for a better-educated work force continues to grow.

There are a number of other considerations, however, that could offset the effects of the decline in the traditional college-age group and that could lead to a moderation in the growth of college charges. First, although enrollment and applicant trends suggest that students and their families were relatively insensitive to tuition increases in the 1980s, basic economic theory suggests that *at some point* higher prices must dampen the demand for a higher education. Many private sector institutions may moderate their tuition increases if they perceive that they have begun to price themselves out of the market. Public concerns about high costs might spur a reform movement that emphasizes teaching over research and greater use of new technologies to achieve productivity gains and a moderation in the cost function. Or institutions faced with a consumer revolt over prices may have to respond by cutting expenditures, albeit with some threat to the quality of the education they provide.

Second, overall economic conditions could have a substantial impact on the pattern of tuition increases in the future. A continued healthy economy should lead to further growth in state funds and a consequent continued moderation in the growth of public tuitions. A recession, however, could lead to a substantial jump in public college charges unless a large number of states shift to formulas in which tuitions are set on the basis of state funding or spending levels. Changing economic conditions tend to have an opposite effect on private sector tuitions. The predominant effect of a good economy is to buoy demand for private higher education, thus leading to higher tuitions, whereas an economic downturn would limit the ability of many families to pay higher tuitions.

Finally, it is possible that the cycle of economic returns to higher education might turn downward again despite the anticipated continued decline in the number of traditional college graduates competing for jobs. The relative economic value of a college education has tended to move in ways that are difficult to predict. A decline in value could have an impact on tuitions if confidence in higher education's product diminishes and institutions become convinced that they must compete on the basis of lower prices rather than with better facilities to attract students.

This study has attempted to shed some light on what existing data tell us about why college charges have increased in the past and what they may do in the future. But without further research and debate, these thoughts contain much speculation about what is a very important but still confusing subject. We hope that this study will point toward a better understanding of why college charges have been increasing rapidly in recent years and of what could be done to reduce that increase in the future.

STATISTICS ON COLLEGE
CHARGES AND EXPENDITURES

TABLE A-1

YEAR TO YEAR CHANGES IN THE HIGHER EDUCATION PRICE INDEX (HEPI) AND CONSUMER PRICE INDEX (CPI), 1961-87

INDEX NUMBERS			ANNUAL CHANGE		
Year	HEPI (1971=100)	CPI (1967=100)	Year	HEPI	CPI
1961	60.4	89.6	1961		
1962	62.5	90.6	1962	3.5%	1.1%
1963	65.0	91.7	1963	4.0%	1.2%
1964	67.4	92.9	1964	3.7%	1.3%
1965	70.3	94.5	1965	4.3%	1.7%
1966	73.8	97.2	1966	5.0%	2.9%
1967	77.7	100.0	1967	5.3%	2.9%
1968	82.4	104.2	1968	6.0%	4.2%
1969	88.0	109.8	1969	6.8%	5.4%
1970	94.0	116.3	1970	6.8%	5.9%
1971	100.0	121.3	1971	6.4%	4.3%
1972	105.6	125.3	1972	5.6%	3.3%
1973	111.2	133.1	1973	5.3%	6.2%
1974	119.1	147.7	1974	7.1%	11.0%
1975	129.2	161.2	1975	8.5%	9.1%
1976	137.8	170.5	1976	6.7%	5.8%
1977	146.8	181.5	1977	6.5%	6.5%
1978	156.6	195.4	1978	6.7%	7.7%
1979	168.7	217.4	1979	7.7%	11.3%
1980	185.3	246.8	1980	9.8%	13.5%
1981	205.2	272.4	1981	10.7%	10.4%
1982	225.8	289.1	1982	10.0%	6.1%
1983	240.1	298.4	1983	6.3%	3.2%
1984	253.0	311.1	1984	5.4%	4.3%
1985	270.1	322.2	1985	6.8%	3.6%
1986	281.9	328.4	1986	4.4%	1.9%
1987	293.6	340.4	1987	4.2%	3.7%

SOURCES: HEPI: Research Associates of Washington, Higher Education Prices and Price Indexes, various years.

CPI: U.S. Department of Labor, Bureau of Labor Statistics.

TABLE A-2

TUITION AND FEES, AND ALL COLLEGE CHARGES, BY TYPE AND CONTROL OF INSTITUTION, 1965-66 TO 1987-88

TUITION AND FEES

	Public				Private			
	2-Year	4-Year	Univ.	All	2-Year	4-Year	Univ.	All
1965-66	109	241	327	257	768	1086	1369	1154
1966-67	121	259	360	275	845	1162	1456	1233
1967-68	144	268	366	283	892	1237	/534	1297
1968-69	170	281	377	295	956	1335	1638	1383
1969-70	178	306	427	323	1034	1468	1809	1533
1970-71	187	332	478	351	1109	1603	1980	1684
1971-72	192	354	526	376	1172	1721	2133	1820
1972-73	233	455	566	407	1221	1846	2226	1898
1973-74	274	463	581	438	1303	1925	2375	1989
1974-75	277	448	599	432	1367	1954	2614	2117
1975-76	245	469	642	433	1427	2084	2881	2272
1976-77	283	564	689	479	1592	2351	3051	2467
1977-78	306	596	736	512	1706	2520	3240	2624
1978-79	327	622	777	543	1831	2771	3487	2867
1979-80	355	662	840	583	2062	3020	3811	3130
1980-81	385	721	915	633	2413	3390	4275	3498
1981-82	432	813	1042	721	2697	3855	4887	3972
1982-83	473	936	1164	798	3008	4329	5583	4439
1983-84	528	1052	1284	891	3099	4726	6217	4851
1984-85	584	1117	1386	971	3485	5135	6843	5314
1985-86	641	1157	1536	1044	3672	5641	7374	5778
1986-87	660	1248	1651	1106	3684	6171	8118	6316
1987-88	690	1320	1750	1160	3910	6670	8770	6820

TABLE A-2 (Continued)

TUITION AND FEES, AND ALL COLLEGE CHARGES, BY TYPE AND CONTROL OF INSTITUTION, 1965-66 TO 1987-88

COLLEGE CHARGES

	Public				Private			
	2-Year	4-Year	Univ.	All	2-Year	4-Year	Univ.	All
1965-66	670	904	1105	983	1557	1899	2316	2005
1966-67	710	947	1171	1026	1679	2007	2456	2124
1967-68	789	997	1199	1064	1762	2104	2545	2205
1968-69	883	1063	1245	1117	1876	2237	2673	2321
1969-70	951	1135	1362	1203	1993	2420	2920	2530
1970-71	998	1206	1477	1287	2103	2599	3163	2738
1971-72	1073	1263	1579	1357	2186	2748	3375	2917
1972-73	1197	1460	1668	1458	2273	2934	3512	3038
1973-74	1274	1506	1707	1517	2410	3040	3717	3164
1974-75	1339	1558	1760	1563	2591	3156	4076	3403
1975-76	1386	1657	1935	1666	2711	3385	4467	3663
1976-77	1490	1828	2066	1789	2971	3714	4716	3907
1977-78	1589	1932	2170	1888	3148	3968	5033	4158
1978-79	1691	2027	2289	1994	3389	4326	5403	4514
1979-80	1821	2198	2487	2165	3755	4699	5888	4912
1980-81	2020	2420	2711	2371	4290	5249	6566	5468
1981-82	2217	2701	3079	2668	4840	5949	7439	6184
1982-83	2390	3032	3403	2944	5364	6646	8537	6920
1983-84	2534	3285	3628	3156	5571	7244	9307	7509
1984-85	2807	3518	3899	3408	6203	7849	10243	8202
1985-86	2981	3637	4146	3584	6512	8551	11034	8868
1986-87	3056	3959	4543	3875	6456	9356	12381	9762
1987-88	3230	4130	4760	4030	6870	10050	13330	10480

NOTE: College Charges include Tuition, Fees, Room, and Board

SOURCE: U.S. Department of Education, *Digest of Education Statistics, 1988.*

TABLE A-3

EDUCATION RELATED EXPENDITURES PER FTE STUDENT, BY TYPE AND CONTROL OF INSTITUTION, 1976-77 TO 1985-86

	Public			
	2-Year	4-Year	University	All
1976-77	2047	3759	5149	3517
1977-78	2213	4068	5561	3797
1978-79	2456	4517	6205	4239
1979-80	2652	5019	6748	4640
1980-81	2816	5508	7355	5019
1981-82	3085	6017	7934	5456
1982-83	3106	6244	8433	5634
1983-84	3304	6619	9038	6005
1984-85	3823	7401	10013	6805
1985-86	4130	8008	10895	7388

	Private			
	2-Year	4-Year	University	All
1976-77	2400	3688	7634	4795
1977-78	2415	3928	8034	5071
1978-79	2707	4279	8765	5534
1979-80	2913	4769	9786	6174
1980-81	3211	5288	10923	6847
1981-82	3429	5861	11931	7517
1982-83	3758	6378	12803	8086
1983-84	3885	6867	14312	8863
1984-85	4500	7478	15704	9718
1985-86	4753	8085	17079	10540

SOURCE: Derived from tables found in U.S. Department of Education, *Digest of Education Statistics, 1988.*

TABLE A-4
TOTAL EXPENDITURES AND EXPENDITURES PER STUDENT
BY CONTROL OF INSTITUTION, 1970-71 TO 1985-86

	CURRENT $			CONSTANT $		
	Public	Private	Total	Public	Private	Total
Total Expenditures, in Millions						
1970-71	14996	8379	23375	42271	23619	65890
1971-72	16484	9075	25560	44003	24225	68228
1972-73	18204	9752	27956	46146	24721	70867
1973-74	20336	10377	30714	48151	24571	72722
1974-75	23490	11568	35058	51234	25230	76464
1975-76	26184	12719	38903	53565	26020	79585
1976-77	28635	13965	42600	55009	26827	81836
1977-78	30725	15246	45971	55330	27454	82784
1978-79	33733	16988	50721	56377	28392	84769
1979-80	37768	19146	56914	57476	29136	86613
1980-81	42280	21773	64053	58077	29908	87985
1981-82	46219	24120	70339	57694	30109	87803
1982-83	49573	26363	75936	58194	30947	89141
1983-84	53087	28907	81993	59139	32202	91342
1984-85	58314	31637	89951	60866	33021	93888
1985-86	63194	34342	97536	63194	34342	97536
Per-Student Expenditures						
1970-71	2970	4606	3403	8534	13235	9779
1971-72	3048	4971	3534	8233	13427	9544
1972-73	3309	5367	3820	8463	13727	9770
1973-74	3521	5546	4017	8553	13472	9757
1974-75	3800	5979	4320	8618	13560	9796
1975-76	3929	6359	4489	8213	13293	9385
1976-77	4420	6974	5023	8663	13669	9845
1977-78	4701	7391	5346	8650	13599	9837
1978-79	5205	7955	5887	8978	13721	10154
1979-80	5616	8688	6374	8991	13910	10205
1980-81	5998	9426	6845	8743	13740	9977
1981-82	6464	10243	7400	8508	13482	9740
1982-83	7102	11544	8197	8495	13809	9805
1983-84	7639	12568	8865	8594	14138	9973
1984-85	8526	13694	9831	9102	14620	10496
1985-86	9471	15187	10918	9471	15187	10918

SOURCE: U.S. Department of Education, *Digest of Education Statistics,* 1988.

RECENT STUDIES, REPORTS, AND DATA SOURCES CONCERNING COLLEGE COSTS AND PRICES

American Council on Education. "Special Focus: The Tuition Battle." *Educational Record* (Spring/Summer 1986): 4-20.

This collection of five articles explores many of the themes currently being considered in the college cost debate. The articles examine differences in cost between institutions, the levels at which tuitions have been rising in recent years, the impact of educational debts on intergenerational equity, the ways of gauging families' ability to pay, and the impact of federal student aid cuts on access to higher education. Together, they explore the variables in exploring college cost increases and the many reasons why some cost increases are out of the control of individual institutions. (The articles by Sheldon Hackney and by Richard Yanikoski are annotated individually below.)

Augustin, James W., and Carol Mishler. "Coping with the Costs: How Adults Pay Their College Expenses." *Journal of Student Financial Aid* (Fall 1986): 4-12.

This study explores the sources that adult degree-seeking students at the University of Wisconsin rely on to finance their educations. Special emphasis is placed on some of the adult-specific expenses related to college costs, such as child care and transportation, as well as books, supplies, and fees. The authors discuss the challenges in meeting the needs of this growing segment of the higher education population.

Berg, D.J., and S.A. Hoenack. "The Concept of Cost-Related Tuition and Its Implementation at the University of Minnesota." *Journal of Higher Education* (May/June 1987): 276-305.

This study details the experience of the University of Minnesota since the implementation of its cost-related tuition program. Cost-related tuition, in which tuition levels vary according to the type of program, academic level of study, and sometimes the courses taken by students, attempts to take into account the nonuniformity of instructional costs across different fields of study. The advantage of this market-based tuition strategy is that it allows institutions to maintain revenues while responding to the demands of student preferences and educational costs. The possible inequities that could occur with such a strategy are also examined.

Bowen, Howard R. *The Costs of Higher Education.* San Francisco: Jossey-Bass, 1980.

This seminal work on higher education costs was written when concerns about educational quality were beginning to reemerge after the relatively stagnant period of the 1970s and when expectations were high that enrollments would decrease rapidly in the 1980s. Bowen begins with an analysis of the determinants of higher education costs and then examines trends both nationally and on an institutional level. Of particular import are the author's analyses of why higher education costs rise faster than costs generally; his historical accounting of the rise and fall of faculty salaries and compensation; his analysis of the significant differences in per-student costs at similar institutions; and his now often-quoted *revenue theory of costs,* best summarized by the axiom that "institutions raise all the money they can and spend all they can raise." The final section looks at what higher education should cost based on the concepts of efficiency, minimum standards, and equity.

Bowen, William G. "The Student Aid-Tuition Nexus." *Higher Education and National Affairs,* May 18, 1987.

Bowen examines the conceptual relationship between increases in federal student aid and increases in tuition, specifically concerning the causal relationship between the two and the consequences of changes in each on educational outcomes. In the case of selective institutions, the author notes, reductions in student aid force institutions to increase their own expenditures to ensure the attendance of a diverse student population. "Need blind" admissions policies encourage students from varying backgrounds to pursue an education, regardless of their financial resources. Less selective institutions have the dual problem of risking enrollment declines and a lack of alternative funding sources when it comes to tuition increases. Thus, reductions in external (federal) aid may not be offset, resulting in increased burdens on all students.

Carnes, Bruce M. "The Campus Cost Explosion." *Policy Review* (Spring 1987): 68-71.

The author argues that several little-discussed trends in higher education have led to higher costs in the past decade. These include the labor-intensivity of teaching, which requires an adequate ratio of teachers to students to ensure maximum quality of instruction; colleges' practice of charging what the market will bear because of the rising demand for higher education; the tendency of institutions to maximize revenues; and the availability of federal student aid. Many of these arguments have been challenged by other analysts.

College Scholarship Service. *The College Cost Book, 1988-89.* **New York: College Entrance Examination Board, 1988.**

This annually updated volume provides essential data on student charges, including tuition and fees, out-of-state charges, costs for books and supplies, and a breakdown of costs for campus residents versus commuters, for some 3,100 colleges and universities. Other information provided on an institution-by-institution basis includes the percentages of freshmen receiving financial aid, the availability of institution-based aid, and the types of innovative financing schemes available. The volume also contains useful financial planning information for families.

Council for Advancement and Support of Education (CASE). *Tuition: The Story and How to Tell It.* **Transcript of a CASE senior seminar, October 13-14, 1987.**

CASE convened a group of college and university officials to discuss the controversy over rising tuitions and how higher education institutions might best respond to it. The group reviewed some of the major factors affecting institutional budgets, current and future trends in institutional costs, how tuition prices are set, and strategies for increasing understanding of the tuition issue both within and outside of the higher education community.

Freund, William H. *Tuitions in Postsecondary Education, 1987-88.* **National Center for Education Statistics Survey Report, Data Series DR-IPEDS-87/88-X.X. Washington, D.C.: U.S. Department of Education, Office of Educational Research and Improvement, January 1989.**

The 1987-88 Institutional Characteristics Survey, part of the Integrated Postsecondary Education Data System (IPEDS), is used to examine the distribution of annual tuitions for full-time students as reported by all of the nation's two-year and four-year higher education institutions. The findings show that very few institutions charge extremely high tuitions. Tuition charges reported by four-year public institutions are much higher for out-of-state students than for in-state students. Further, the study shows differences in tuitions by school size and geographic location (highest tuitions were in the Northeast).

Greenberg, Marvin W. "What's Happened to College Tuitions and Why: A View from the Public University." *The College Board Review* **(Spring 1988): 13 + .**

The author contends that recent tuition jumps at public institutions have been caused by accumulated deficits from the 1970s, the need for qualitative improvements in academic programs, and other factors. The article stresses the costs of the "knowledge explosion" to public institutions. High technology, automation, libraries, and instructional laboratories and equipment all have pushed the need to raise tuitions sharply. Cost containment, the author argues, must become the most important consideration to prevent unnecessary price increases.

Hackney, Sheldon. "Under the Gun: Why College Is So Expensive." *Educational Record* **(Spring/Summer 1986): 9-10.**

Often lost in the fretting over high college prices is the fact that tuitions do not cover all of the costs of education for an average institution. This article is a college president's look at how those costs can vary considerably from school to school. Where the institution is located, how extensive its research facilities are, what its specific academic mission is, and whether it is a public or private school are some of the reasons cited for cost differences and therefore for significant variations in price.

Halstead, Kent. *Higher Education Tuition.* **Washington, D.C.: Research Associates of Washington, 1989.**

The author uses historical, current, and projected statistics to explain the role of student charges in American higher education. The book explores diverse topics, including the range of institutions and prices available to students, inflation and its effect on college costs, tuition-setting policies, the reasons for escalating costs, and the level of savings required to meet projected tuition increases.

Hardesty, Sarah, *What People Are Saying About College Prices and College Costs,* **Council for Advancement and Support of Education, 1989**

This compendium was written to provide campus officials with an overview of the various studies and articles on the issue of college costs and tuitions. Sections include research on the level of tuitions, different ways of paying for college, the components of college spending, and what colleges are doing to contain their costs. It includes a bibliography on each section, as well as reprints of a number of relevant articles.

Hansen, W. Lee, and Jacob S. Stampen. *Balancing Quality and Access in Financing Higher Education.* **Research report, National Center for Postsecondary Governance and Finance, September 1987.**

This report suggests that a trade-off has occurred in the last four decades between quality and access in higher education. The authors show a parallelism between measures of higher education expenditures and the net student share of these expenditures. The data show that instruction-related costs per student (a measure of quality) increased measurably between the late 1940s and early 1970s but declined steadily through 1981. In the 1980s, per-student instruction costs have increased moderately, but governmental and voluntary contributions increased more slowly. As a result, recent efforts at improving quality have been largely funded by higher tuition charges, which have not been offset fully by increases in institutionally funded student aid.

Harford, J.D. and R.D. Marcus. **"Tuition and U.S. Private College Characteristics: The Hedonic Approach."** *Economics of Education Review* **no. 4 (1986): 415-30.**

This study looks at data from more than six hundred private four-year colleges that offer a wide range of liberal arts courses. Tuitions are compared with several variables, with regression showing that higher tuitions are correlated with higher SAT scores, smaller populations of black students, variety of programs offered, library resources, and larger residential student populations. These trends are partially explained by regional variations.

Hauptman, Arthur, and Terry Hartle.   "Tuition Increases Since 1970: A Perspective." *Higher Education and National Affairs,* **February 23, 1987.**

The authors examine trends in tuitions from 1970 to 1986, compared to the growth in prices for other goods and services as well as measures of income. They find that since 1970 tuition has increased about one percentage point per year faster than consumer prices. By educational sector, private institutions have experienced more rapid increases than public schools.   Overall tuition has increased more slowly than medical care, housing, and energy but more rapidly than food and new car prices. Several hypotheses for escalating tuitions since 1980 are offered. These include rapid increases in faculty salaries in this decade, declining availability of federal student aid, and the ability of elite institutions to raise prices without an appreciable impact on demand.

Henderson, Cathy.   "Looking Ahead at Student Expenses." *Academe,* **October/November 1988**

This article presents data on tuitions and other student charges from 1978-79 to 1988-89 and makes projections for these charges through 1990-91   The author finds that factors that have caused institutions to raise their tuitions at higher-than-inflation rates will be sustained for the immediate future. The increasing demands placed on institutional budgets by faculty salaries, the declining purchasing power of federal student aid, and recent efforts to improve educational quality are all cited as reasons why many institutions will be forced to continue to raise their student charges at rates higher than general inflation increases.

Higher Education Coordinating Board, State of Washington. *1987 Tuition and Fee Rates: A National Comparison.* **Olympia: State of Washington, February 1988.**

This data report of tuition and fee rates at public institutions in all fifty states has been produced annually for the past two decades. The report contains data on tuition and fee rates for full-time resident and nonresident undergraduate and graduate students back to 1968-69. Four-year and colleges and universities and two-year community colleges are covered in this basic source document.

Higher Education Research Program Sponsored by The Pew Charitable Trusts, "Double Trouble," *Policy Perspectives,* **September 1989, Volume 2, Number 1**

This essay describes a number of the considerations that are factored into the tuition-setting process. It argues that a major reason why tuitions have been increasing is that too many colleges and universities are relying on a cost-plus pricing model. It provides a number of suggestions for how colleges and universities can rein in their costs and tuitions including setting revenues first and learning to grow by substitution. The report also includes a distillation of other commentaries and studies including a very helpful analysis of trends and expenditures in the 1980s at seven different types of institutions.

Johnstone, D. Bruce. *Sharing the Costs of Higher Education: Student Financial Assistance in the United Kingdom, the Federal Republic of Germany, France, Sweden, and the United States.* **New York: College Entrance Examination Board, 1986.**

This book examines some of the issues affecting student financial assistance in five Western nations. For each, the author looks at the structure and governance of its higher education system, the costs passed on to students and their families, the abilities of parents and students to meet these costs, and the organization of the various financial assistance programs. The import of these cross-national trends on the analysis and practice of financial assistance in the United States receives special attention.

Johnstone, D. Bruce. **"The 'Crisis' in College Costs: Unenlightened and Boring."** *Higher Education and National Affairs,* **April 11, 1988.**

With the annual flurry of activity surrounding tuition increases, the author (a college president) attempts to put these concerns in perspective by noting that the most institutions do not have the "crises" in rising tuitions that many newspapers and magazines decry. The author suggests that rising costs, although important, should not distract institutions from concentrating on equally vexing issues, such as student retention, curriculum reform, and teacher evaluation.

Kuttner, Robert. "The Patrimony Society." *The New Republic,* **May 11, 1987, pp. 18-21.**

This article explores the broader theme of intergenerational equity in the context of rising costs for housing and college. The author argues that potential home buyers or college students who have the benefit of significant parental support are at a significant advantage compared with those who lack such assistance. He asserts that a "level playing field" of economic opportunity is not possible if federal policy reinforces the notion that the social class of parents can dictate the economic prospects of their children.

Lee, John B. *The Equity in Higher Education Subsidies.* **Research report. Washington, D.C.: National Center for Postsecondary Governance and Finance, June 1987.**

Data from the 1980 High School and Beyond longitudinal study are used in combination with institutional survey data to analyze where subsidies are targeted. The author finds that the proportion of students attending college increases with increasing family income and higher ability. The total subsidy (from all sources) was greater for students with a family income under $12,000 for both 1980 and 1983, but students from higher income backgrounds received larger institutional subsidies. By race, Asian and black students received the largest total subsidies, whereas Hispanic and native American students received the least. Top-ability students were the recipients of more subsidy than lower-ability students.

Leslie, Larry L., and Paul T. Brinkman. *The Economic Value of Higher Education.* **New York: ACE/MacMillan, 1988.**

This book uses meta-analysis--essentially a methodology that average the results of various studies on a particular subject--to measure higher education's economic value and to determine whether it is a "good investment." The authors examine studies on the economics of higher education going back several decades on issues such as the economic impact of colleges on local communities, the rates of return to higher education, the effect of tuition increases on enrollment, and the effects of student aid on college going decisions. The authors conclude that higher education has an important impact on the nation's economic viability, and is of critical importance to local economies, students, educational institutions, and society in general. Also useful is the extensive bibliography compiled to perform the meta-analysis.

Ludwig, Meredith, and Gerald Kress. *Student Charges at Public Institutions: Annual Survey 1988-89.* **Washington, D.C.: American Association of State Colleges and Universities/National Association of State Universities and Land-Grant Colleges, 1989.**

This data report describes the costs of attending about 90 percent of the nation's four-year public colleges and universities. The report includes an institution-by-institution breakdown of student charges for both resident and nonresident students at the undergraduate, graduate, and first professional levels. Enrollment pressures and improved housing for students are also explored as issues affecting campus finances.

McNamee, Mike. "Behind the Great Tuition Debate." *Currents* **(October 1988): 24-30.**

This article, published in the magazine of the Council for Advancement and Support of Education (CASE), argues that economic and social conditions are the true source of anxiety about college costs. The author contends that higher education has argued its case for tuitions rising above the level of inflation on the wrong grounds, citing institutional needs rather than uncontrollable economic and social factors. The article notes that tuition increases in the last two decades have averaged just one percentage point above inflation and have been smaller than gains in income, but that public opinion polls show that people estimate the average cost of a year in college at almost twice its true level.

McPherson, Michael S. and Mary S. Skinner. "Paying for College: A Lifetime Proposition." *The Brookings Review* **(Fall 1986): 29-36.**

Current higher education financing and student aid trends are analyzed in this article as a way of exploring the issue of intergenerational equity in paying for college. Of particular concern to the authors is how the burden of college finance is shared between generations. They note that "the arrangement of having each generation pay for its successor works only so long as every generation honors the implicit agreement to perpetuate the chain." The recent trend toward greater reliance on loans--which, obviously, upsets the balance by shifting a significant portion of the burden onto the generation that is in school--

has important implications for the future of American higher education policy. The authors contend that the nation must decide how this burden is to be shared in order to preserve the existing generational compact. Considerable concern is expressed for the growing plight of needy students and for the importance of considering them in the financing picture.

National Center for Postsecondary Governance and Finance *College Costs and Tuition: What Are the Issues? Proceedings from a National Conference.* **Washington, D.C.: , January 20, 1988.**

Representatives from higher education institutions, policy analysts, and policymakers met to discuss the escalation of college costs and tuition. This report summarizes that meeting and the papers delivered by six experts on higher education finance including Paul Brinkman, Dennis Curry, W. Lee Hansen, and Arthur Hauptman. The meeting explored several diverse issues, including issues in the debate over higher education cost increases (the use of inflation rates and indices, historical trends, etc.); problems involved with measuring costs; the effects of student aid on price increases; and cost containment in higher education and its parallels in health care. It was also at this meeting that David Breneman first publicly discussed his concerns about how many institutions were setting their tuitions, and the notion that students and their parents were confusing price with quality, what he termed the "Chivas Regal effect."

National Institute of Independent Colleges and Universities (NIICU). *The Truth About Costs in the Independent Sector of Higher Education.* **Washington, D.C.: NIICU, 1987.**

This short report looks exclusively at the costs that independent colleges and universities face in educating their students. Differences between college prices-- what the student and family pay--versus college costs--what it costs an institution to educate the student--are discussed. Reasons cited to account for the disparity between cost increases and inflation include higher faculty salaries, increasing insurance costs, the declining value of governmental assistance, skyrocketing costs of goods and equipment, and a greater emphasis on campus services.

O'Keefe, Michael. "College Costs: Have They Gone Too High Too Fast?" *Change* (May/June 1986): 6-8.

This commentary focuses on the hidden transfers in higher education pricing policies. The discounting of higher education prices for some students shifts the burden to others, resulting in substantial inequities. As institutional student aid increased in recent years, middle-income students are being forced to pay a larger share of the costs associated with the goals of equal opportunity. With the rise of merit scholarships, less-qualified students are increasingly supporting those more academically proficient. And undergraduate students appear to be paying more and more of their tuitions to support the work of graduate students and faculty, especially at larger research universities. The author contends that these cross-subsidies are worsening the inequities between groups of students, and he suggests that society must work with colleges and universities to support the ongoing goals of access and choice for all students.

O'Keefe, Michael. "Where Does the Money Really Go? Case Studies of Six Institutions." *Change* (November/December 1987): 12-34.

This examination of expenditures between 1976 and 1986 compares the similarities and marked differences between six different institutions, and the challenges each faces at controlling costs and prices. Although noting the uniqueness of each school, the author distills several cross-institutional trends. Significant increases in administrative costs at all six schools are cited as important contributors to the growth in costs. So, too, are efforts to improve the quality of research and instruction, an important trend at all of the schools. Competition between schools is also held responsible for some of the higher expenditures, particularly for costs associated with admission and recruitment.

Snyder, Thomas P., and Eva Galambos. *Higher Education Administrative Costs: Continuing the Study.* Washington, D.C.: U.S. Department of Education, Office of Educational Research and Improvement, January 1988.

This two-part publication looks first at trends in higher education finance since 1976-77. HEGIS data on tuition, enrollments, degrees, and expenditures are compared, showing shifts in these measures over the last ten years. Second, the study examines higher education administrative costs over four decades using three data sources: national data series, state higher education agency reports, and two institutional case studies. Increased administrative costs are noted in the 1960s and early 1970s, with a creeping increase noted in the early 1980s.

To, Duc-Le. *Estimating the Cost of a Bachelor's Degree: An Institutional Cost Analysis.* **Washington, D.C.: U.S. Department of Education, Office of Educational Research and Improvement, 1987.**

This study estimates the institutional costs of a bachelor's degree and compares these costs among different types of institutions. The author finds that in 1983 institutional costs of a degree were as much as $10,000 higher at private institutions. The report includes an appendix of comments from higher education financing experts who question various dimensions of the author's analysis, most significantly the use of student financial assistance as a cost of undergraduate instruction.

U.S. House of Representatives, Subcommittee on Postsecondary Education. *Hearings on Higher Education Costs,* **serial no. 100-47. Washington, D.C.: U.S. Government Printing Office, 1988.**

This committee print compiles both the prepared statements and actual testimony of about twenty witnesses at a hearing held on September 15, 1987. The subcommittee heard from a diverse group of speakers on the many reasons behind rising college costs. The witnesses included William Bowen, Douglass Cater, Chester Finn, Kenneth Green, Arthur Hauptman,and Julianne Still-Thrift.

Warner, Timothy R. "College Costs: A View from the Private University." *The College Board Review* **(Spring 1988): 16+ .**

The factors that have an impact on how tuitions are set at Stanford University is explored in this article by the university's budget director. The author uses a simplified operating budget and projected annual real long-term growth rates to demonstrate the "two percent" problem at Stanford--the fact that the difference between projected income and base line expenditures typically comes to 2 percent and requires further adjustments during the budgeting process. Program improvements are the main reason cited for escalating prices.

Weber, Arnold R., "Colleges Must Begin Weighing Public Perceptions, as Well as Economic Reality, When Setting Tuition," October 11, 1989: A52

This commentary, which is drawn from a longer speech delivered at the Assembly of Council for Advancement of Education in July 1989, urges college presidents and others to reexamine their thinking about why college tuitions are increasing and what can be done about it. Weber argues that students and their parents no longer buy the traditional arguments for higher tuitions, for good reason The arguments are too complex and do not fully reflect the reality of how tuitions are set. He concludes with a plea that colleges moderate their future tuition increases.

Werth, Barry. "Why Is College So Expensive?" *New England Monthly* **(January 1988): 35-44.**

This piece, reprinted in the March/April 1988 issue of *Change*, tells about college cost increases and "the irreducible imperatives of Big Money" at Mount Holyoke College in Massachusetts. The college, which increased its tuition by 110 percent between 1980 and 1987, is used as a case study of cost increases and the pressures of market competitiveness on private institutions. The author contends that the institution's focused efforts to improve the quality of the students and the education they receive has come about largely because of a "Chivas Regal" mentality--a conceding to public perceptions that price increases are equated with quality.

Yanikoski, Richard A. "Over a Barrel: The High Cost of Rising Tuitions." *Educational Record* **(Spring/Summer 1986): 12-15.**

Based in part on the author's research on differential pricing in higher education, this article explores the possible cumulative impact of high college price increases over several years. Of concern to the author are the probable impact on enrollments of a series of large price increases, the problems associated with high debt levels for the current generation on future generations, and the tendency of some institutions to use "tuition discounting" to attract prospective students for undersubscribed programs of study.